Praise for *Visionary*

I can say with conviction: this book is the essential sequel to *Rocket Fuel*. Every Visionary needs it. If you are sitting in the Visionary seat, you cannot afford to skip this book. It is not optional. It is your operating manual.

—Gino Wickman
Author of *Traction*, Creator of EOS,
and Co-Author of *Rocket Fuel*

A must-read for founders who want to scale fast, stay true to their vision, and enjoy the ride. *Visionary* nails the real journey of being an entrepreneur—that constant pull between wanting to grow and wanting to be free. Mark shows founders how to scale up their business and their life without losing themselves along the way. Every entrepreneur should read this!

—Brian Scudamore
Founder and CEO of 1-800-GOT-JUNK?
and O2E Brands

Visionary is the kind of book every entrepreneur like me needs. It's not about doing more; it's about doing what only you can do. Mark lays out the 10 Pillars that help Visionaries stay focused, healthy, and in their zone of genius while building unstoppable teams. This book gives real, practical tools to create freedom without losing your fire. If you've ever felt torn between big dreams and daily chaos, this one will hit home.

—Tommy Mello
CEO & Founder of A1 Garage Door Service

There's no better way to understand yourself—your roses and your thorns—than leading others into greatness. In *Visionary*, Mark captures how Visionaries see things, run things, and why we might destroy things just to make something better. With Winters' new book and his deep understanding of this unique creature in its own habitat, the Visionary's journey can be more than just an exercise in self-expression; it can be the ultimate growth experience.

—Lewis Schiff
Chairman, Birthing of Giants Fellowship program

If you aren't so lucky (as I was) to have Mark's coaching in person to help make you the best Visionary you can be, then this book is the next best thing. Get it, read it, embrace it, and go for it!

—Eve Mayer
New York Times Bestselling Author,
Mentor for Women Entrepreneurs

Rocket Fuel helped us harness our V/I relationship super-power. It gave shape to what had once been instinct and friction. And now, *Visionary* takes that understanding to an even deeper level—helping those of us wired this way to reflect, focus, and refine our practice of leadership.

Even with an Integrator by your side, the Visionary seat can be an odd and lonely place, filled with endless pressure and boundless possibility. *Visionary* makes that daily work of improvement and alignment not only possible but clear. It's a book I wish I'd had years ago. Every founder, creative, or entrepreneurial leader who feels "too much" for traditional structures will see themselves in these pages—and find a way to build something greater, with more clarity, freedom, and joy.

Mark makes the impossible balance of creativity and structure feel achievable, and the Visionary journey less lonely. *Visionary* turns entrepreneurial chaos into clarity—structure for the creative mind and focus for the fearless founder.

—David Kaplan
Founder & CEO of Death & Co

Visionary is the book I didn't know I needed. But Mark put a mirror in front of me, and the truth was undeniable: I am a Visionary. I'd been in denial, and this book gave me the clarity and freedom to finally own who I am. Page after page, I found myself having light bulb moments. Mark captures both the power and pitfalls of being a Visionary in a way that is relatable and practical. This book helped me stop resisting how I'm wired and instead lean into it, collaborate more effectively, and move forward with clarity about my role.

—Ann Sheu
Founder and CEO, Mpowered Journey

Visionary captures my five-year transformation with Mark as my guide. Before Mark, I was drowning. I tried to do everything myself—no days off, constant deadlines, endless papers and presentations across the country. The business was consuming my life while growing at a crawl.

Everything changed when I hired an Integrator and began working with Mark. Over the next five years, my revenue grew at a 30% compound annual growth rate, culminating in an eight-figure exit in year five. The paradox? My company performed better with me doing less. Only then could I finally enjoy my life. This guide gives you the roadmap to achieve your own vision.

—Ronald G. Johnsey
Co-Founder and Chairman of the Board, LaborIQ.co

Being a visionary is like having a superpower—and Mark's *Visionary* is the ultimate guide to mastering it. This is a must-read for any Visionary who wants to channel their power constructively, create maximum impact, and avoid the destructive consequences that can come with it. Mark brilliantly offers practical and action-able tools to tackle complex, emotional, and ego-level challenges, making this book a true hands-on manual. What I love most is how it speaks to the Visionary as an individual—not just as a business leader. This book doesn't just make you a better Visionary; it helps you build a better life. And as Visionaries, we don't like being told what to do—Mark completely gets that. He empowers, offering choices and freedom throughout the book to design our own ideal visionary life.

—Indu Sanka
CEO, Red Elephant

In just a few short years, Mark has helped our company grow 6x while enjoying more personal freedom than at any other point in my life. The wisdom contained in these pages is destined to be a game-changer for all who read and apply these pillars.

—John F. Burns, Jr.
CEO, Exencial Wealth Advisors

I've known Mark for more than a decade, and he's one of the best coaches I've ever known. What makes him great isn't theory—it's how he helps founders cut through noise, face reality, and build something that actually works. *Visionary* is Mark at his best: brutally clear, deeply practical, and grounded in truth earned the hard way.

This isn't a pep talk. It's a playbook for founders who see the future before everyone else but keep getting trapped trying to do it all themselves. Mark shows you how to stop being the bottleneck, build the right kind of partnership, and finally create freedom through structure.

Mark doesn't coddle Visionaries—he shows us how to grow up without giving up what makes us great. He's a world-class teacher and an even better human being. I'm proud to call him a dear friend.

—Mark Abbott
Founder/CEO Ninety

Visionary is a must-read for every entrepreneur who wants to build with clarity, purpose, and freedom. This book reminds us that great leadership isn't about doing it all yourself, but about trusting your team, staying grounded in faith, and leading with conviction. A powerful guide for anyone ready to grow their business and influence.

—Carlos Vaz
CEO of CONTI Capital

Rocket Fuel ignited the blaze that launched my transformation in 2020. I rose fast, burned hot, and nearly lost it all. *Visionary* is the guide for how to rise again—wiser, lighter, and free. For every founder who's ever built something great and then watched the flames get too close—this book is your map through the fire.

—Benny Fisher
Visionary Navigator, Host of
The Big Fish Cares Podcast

Visionary turns ambition into structure—helping founders translate complex innovation into clarity, accountability, and measurable results. If you're a Visionary who's built momentum but craves structure, this book is the bridge. Mark shows you how to keep your creativity intact while building the systems that make it scale. It's the manual every founder eventually realizes they need.

—Will Rosellini
CEO, Darrow Industries

Mark understands Visionaries in a way that feels deeply personal. As I read *Visionary*, I found myself nodding, reflecting, and feeling truly seen. Mark's Ten Pillars offer wise, heartfelt encouragement for those of us who dream big and care deeply about our teams and organizations.

I've helped hundreds of Visionaries and Coaches walk this path—and Mark's words resonate with every challenge and triumph along the way. His insights remind me that knowing ourselves, caring for our spirit, and surrounding ourselves with the right people matter just as much as Vision and Traction!

This book doesn't just guide Visionaries; it lifts us up. Mark's insight, honesty, and experience shine on every page. If you lead with heart and hope for a brighter future, *Visionary* will be the companion you cherish.

—Jill Young
Expert EOS Implementer, Creator of Coaching Magic, Former Head Coach of EOS Worldwide

Mark knows entrepreneurs because he's spent decades in the trenches with them. His *Visionary* framework nails both the brilliance and the blind spots of leaders who build and drive companies. If you want to grow your business without losing yourself in the process, this book is the roadmap.

Mark understands entrepreneurs at a level few do—their drive, their restlessness, and the constant tension between freedom and control. In *Visionary*, he distills that experience into clear, practical guidance for anyone leading from the front. The lessons are honest, hard-won, and field-tested with real companies. For founders and CEOs who want to scale without burning out, this book delivers the structure and insight you need to do it right.

—Mike Sullivan
CEO, The LOOMIS Agency

Why read this book? Because it's the real deal. *Visionary* advances Mark's life work, building upon *Rocket Fuel's* foundation. This book simplifies what it takes to become a great Visionary while providing readers with clarity of purpose and best practice tools. There is no better time than now to read this book. *Visionary* is a "must share"—helping visionaries to "Build something bigger. Something beyond themselves."

—Mike Sterlacci
Founder of CoVerica, CoVerica Agency Alliance, CoVerica Cares, Karis Enterprises Inc., Lotus, and Founding Partner with Ansel Solutions

Finally—a playbook that honors the Visionary spark and protects the team that has to deliver it. *Visionary* is the missing manual for founders who want growth without the people carnage. Mark translates the Visionary/ Integrator dynamic into practical habits that elevate leaders, strengthen culture, and put the right people in the right seats. If you care about talent, execution, and healthy scaling, start here. As a CEO and talent strategist, I live where vision meets execution—and where culture either accelerates or breaks. *Visionary* is the most practical field guide I've read for turning founder energy into healthy, repeatable results. Mark moves beyond inspiration into clear frameworks. The result? Less organizational whiplash, stronger managers, clearer accountability, and a company where top performers want to stay. If you want rocket fuel without burning out your people, read this book and put it to work.

—Jonathan Reynolds
CEO, Titus Talent Strategies

Mark has written *THE* book for Visionaries. He shares the process, structure, and thinking required not only to succeed as a visionary entrepreneur, but to build a life of growth. More than a read, it's a workbook to help you focus and maximize your vision. With *Visionary*, Mark provides the system visionaries need—process, structure, and tools—to focus their energy, elevate their impact, and close the gap between leadership intent and team execution.

—Christopher Turner
Founder & CEO, Emergicon

For every Founder/Owner, this is a must-read! Mark's insights and perspectives are not just theoretical but have been informed by thousands of interactions with Visionaries and their teams over the years. This will become one of a handful of go-to desk references I keep close by.

—Scott Wood
CEO and Co-Founder, True North Advisors

Visionary is a masterclass in the architecture of entrepreneurship. Mark gives structure to what most founders experience as chaos, the tension between imagination and implementation. His 10 Pillars are a practical blueprint for freeing the Visionary to operate from their highest energy and purpose. *Visionary* is the guidebook every founder needs to design not just their company, but the Life it makes possible.

Mark redefines entrepreneurial freedom. *Visionary* shows founders how to convert chaos into clarity, build rhythm with their Integrator, and lead from energy instead of exhaustion. It is a practical blueprint for designing a business that works and a Life that thrives

A timeless guide to transforming entrepreneurial energy into freedom, flow, and sustainable impact without burnout.

—Ninad Tipnas,
Founder & Principal, JTCPL Designs

Mark helps you look at things in new ways, with greater insight. In *Visionary*, his understanding of how Visionaries are wired and his deep experience coaching them shine through with power and clarity. His 10 Pillars are simple, easily understood, and practical. They are inspirational and engaging as well as challenging. *Visionary* will help any visionary leader who sees that their best is still in front of them.

—Tony Caldwell
Co-Founder, Chairman, and CEO, OAA, and
Chairman, Prism Bank

What a treat to read this book! It's very accessible for a Visionary, and incredibly valuable. It helps the reader *see and feel the soul of a Visionary on a deeper level.* There's empathy and understanding, and a clear game plan for us "misfit toys."

As a long-time friend and fellow Visionary, Mark has an endless passion for helping entrepreneurs get unstuck and begin living their ideal lives. *Visionary* is an accessible and practical blueprint for helping you do just that. As a tireless learner and an imperfect entrepreneur, I continuously return to the 10 Pillars as a tangible road map and simple checklist to help me continue on my endless path to mastery and to becoming the best version of myself. I highly recommend this book... but only if you get distracted easily, create chaos, are a genius with 1,000 helpers, think out loud, sometimes feel alone, are often perceived as unrealistic, are a creator, an inventor, a problem solver, and so forth.... ;)

—Alex Freytag
Creator of ProfitWorks®, Expert EOS Implementer,
Author of *Vision Works*, *Profit Works*,
and *Stretch Not Snap*

Mark has an incredible gift for helping entrepreneurs channel their energy and ideas into meaningful, lasting impact. *Visionary* is more than a book; it's a mirror for those of us who have spent our lives building, creating, and leading from the front. Mark understands the inner tension of being a Visionary: the drive to create something extraordinary and the chaos that often follows when we try to do it all ourselves.

Through years of working with founders and leaders, he's distilled what it truly means to lead with purpose, clarity, and discipline. The 10 Pillars he outlines aren't abstract ideals but rather a practical operating system for freedom and focus. Reading this book felt like having a trusted advisor remind me where my energy belongs, and how to build systems and relationships that amplify rather than drain it.

Mark has a rare understanding of one of the most valuable and misunderstood roles in any company: the Visionary. His insights have personally helped me focus my attention, sharpen my vision, and lead more intentionally. If you're a founder or creative leader seeking to build something enduring, without burning yourself out, *Visionary* will give you the roadmap.

Mark understands what it's like to carry a vision too big to do alone. *Visionary* is the field guide every founder needs and has equal parts clarity, wisdom, and practicality.

Mark reveals the path from chaos to clarity by helping visionaries lead with focus, build with purpose, and create lasting impact without doing it all themselves.

—Piyush Patel, Ph.D.
Bestselling Author of *Lead Your Tribe, Love Your Work*, Former CEO of Digital-Tutors

I've worked with Mark for years, and his insight has completely changed how I lead and think. When I first read *Rocket Fuel*, it gave me language and structure for how my company could grow without relying on me to do everything. *Visionary* takes that impact even further. This book speaks directly to leaders who love building, dreaming, and pushing forward but often find themselves carrying the entire weight of their business. Mark shows how to lead with more clarity, less chaos, and far greater freedom. He lays out a practical roadmap to protect your energy, empower your team, and focus on what truly matters.

What makes this book so powerful is that Mark isn't just sharing ideas—he's lived this. He's guided entrepreneurs like me through the real challenges of growth, leadership, and letting go. Reading *Visionary* felt like having Mark sitting across the table, coaching me through the next level. If you're a Visionary who wants to keep building something great without burning yourself out in the process, this is the book you've been waiting for.

Rocket Fuel built the foundation, and *Visionary* changed the game. It's honest, practical, and deeply personal. Every entrepreneur who wants to grow their business and themselves at the same time should read this book. It's clarity, freedom, and leadership wisdom in one.

—Glen Smith
Founder & CEO, GDS Wealth Management

In *Visionary*, Mark provides all of us visionaries a toolkit to not only survive, but thrive. While the 10 Pillars and associated tools include valuable insights and practical applications, reading a book written by an accomplished visionary on how other visionaries can be even better comes with an unexpected benefit: we are not alone. Often, the role of the Visionary can be a lonely experience. Mark provides expert guidance based on decades of experience coaching Visionaries. I look forward to putting these new tools to work in our businesses—and have a new book to discuss in my mastermind group.

—Darin M. Klemchuk
CEO of Klemchuk PLLC and Co-Founder of
Engage Workspace for Lawyers

Mark has spent many years working with and studying Visionaries, and it shows. The role of the Visionary is often misunderstood—sometimes even by the Visionaries themselves—but Mark does an excellent job of clearly defining what it means to be a Visionary and how we can continue to grow as leaders. I especially love the *Intrinsic Genius* exercise—it truly is genius!

—Bob Shenefelt
Founder of iMatter™ & The Visionary Forum

This is the perfect follow-up to *Rocket Fuel*. It is a must-read for leaders who want more freedom and to be the best version of themselves.

—Brad Croy
President, CMP Corporation

To quote Steve Jobs, "Here's to the crazy ones, the misfits, the rebels, the troublemakers, the round pegs in the square holes...." If you are a Visionary, you understand this in your inner being; you "think differently." In *Visionary*, Mark understands us and helps direct us towards being the best we can be. Mark recognizes that "crazy" is a two-way street. The Visionary needs this book to point us down the path to the "good kind of crazy" that really can change the world.

—David Stocker
Founding Partner, SHM Architecture

The learning curve as a Visionary has been steep. There was no textbook, no "how-to" manual—and at times, it's been a lonely and even unsettling journey. *Visionary* has already proven to be an invaluable guide—both a validation of the Visionary experience and a practical roadmap to help avoid many of the inevitable pitfalls along the way (some of which, I'll admit, have been costly and humbling lessons for me). I'm thrilled this book is finally here. *Visionary* has already earned its place as an essential part of my library, as the perfect companion for the entrepreneurial journey. Mark captures the real challenges Visionaries face and offers the roadmap we've all been waiting for. This book is an essential resource for anyone walking the Visionary path. Whether you're new to EOS or a seasoned leader, this book belongs in your library.

—John Sebastian
CEO / Visionary, Sebastian Construction Group

Mark doesn't just describe the Visionary experience—he gives you a practical roadmap to bring the dream inside you to life. *Visionary* isn't just a book—it's a tool for building the future you see. Every Visionary entrepreneur needs this book.

—JoBen Barkey
Founder & Visionary, Soccer Shots
(Orange County & Oahu), Founder, B7 Foundation

Mark articulates the power of the Visionary role in driving entrepreneurial success. By clarifying when to lean in and when to lean on the Integrator, *Visionary* provides the groundwork to leverage your vision and continuously push forward with new ideas.

—Matt Strong
President and Founder, C1S Group, Inc.

Mark has a rare ability to blend deep strategic thinking with genuine care for the entrepreneurial spirit. *Visionary* captures that same balance—it's both practical and profoundly human. This book is Mark at his best: clear, direct, and purpose-driven. He knows the heart and the chaos of the Visionary because he's lived it, coached it, and mastered it. Every page reflects his years of experience helping leaders find clarity, freedom, and impact without losing themselves in the process.

If you're a founder or leader who constantly feels pulled in too many directions, *Visionary* will feel like sitting down with a trusted friend who truly gets you—and knows how to help you channel your energy into something extraordinary.

—Chris White
Founder of The Micro Business Academy and
Author of *The Clarity Playbook*

VISIONARY

*How Driven Entrepreneurs Get
What They Want Without
Doing It All Themselves*

VISIONARY

*How Driven Entrepreneurs Get
What They Want Without
Doing It All Themselves*

**The 10 Pillars of Greatness
That Will Make Your Vision a Reality**

MARK C. WINTERS

E⬡S
IMPACT

Printed in the United States of America

Published by Igniting Souls
PO Box 43, Powell, OH 43065
IgnitingSouls.com

Paperback ISBN: 978-1-63680-577-1
Hardback ISBN: 978-1-63680-578-8
eBook ISBN: 978-1-63680-585-6

Available in paperback, hardcover, e-book, and audiobook.

Any Internet addresses (websites, blogs, etc.) and telephone numbers printed in this book are offered as a resource. They are not intended in any way to be or imply an endorsement by Igniting Souls, nor does Igniting Souls vouch for the content of these sites and numbers for the life of this book.

Some names and identifying details may have been changed to protect the privacy of individuals.

EOS®, The Entrepreneurial Operating System®, Traction®, and EOS Implementer® are registered trademarks owned by EOS Worldwide, LLC. For a complete list of trademarks owned by EOS Worldwide throughout this book, please visit branding.eosworldwide.com/eos-trademarks/.

Kolbe A™ Index is a trademark of Kathy Kolbe. Unique Ability® is a registered trademark of Strategic Coach, Inc. Other third party trademarks, including, but not limited to, Culture Index™, CliftonStrengths®, and The 6 Types of Working Genius® are owned by their respective owners.

The content of this book reflects the author's personal experiences, opinions, and interpretations. The inclusion of any individual, living or deceased, or any organization or entity, is not intended to malign, defame, or harm the reputation of such persons or entities. All statements regarding individuals are solely the author's perspective and do not represent verified facts unless expressly cited to a verifiable source.

The publisher has not independently investigated or confirmed the accuracy of any such references and disclaims all responsibility for them. Nothing in this book should be construed as factual assertions about the character, conduct, or reputation of any individual or entity mentioned. Any resemblance to persons living or dead is purely coincidental unless explicitly stated.

The publisher expressly disclaims liability for any alleged loss, damage, or injury arising from any perceived defamatory content or reliance upon statements within this work. Responsibility for the views, depictions, and representations rests solely with the author.

The superscript symbol IP listed throughout this book is known as the unique certification mark created and owned by Instant IP^{IP}. Its use signifies that the corresponding expression (words, phrases, chart, graph, etc.) has been protected by Instant IP^{IP} via smart contract. Instant IP^{IP} is designed with the patented smart contract solution (US Patent: 11,928,748), which creates an immutable time-stamped first layer and fast layer identifying the moment in time an idea is filed on the blockchain. This solution can be used in defending intellectual property protection. Infringing upon the respective intellectual property, i.e., IP, is subject to and punishable in a court of law.

Dedication

To my mother, Joyce Winters. For always encouraging me. When I got knocked down, you were there to pick me up, dust me off, and send me back out there. The hugs helped too.

To my wife, Beth. For sticking with me through all the ups and downs—even though you had no idea what kind of "entrepreneurial thrill ride" you signed up for. Life is better together.

To my boys, Austin, Blake, and Carson… "the brothers." You are the best part of my own personal vision. I'm blessed to have a front-row seat as each of you makes your own vision a reality.

TABLE OF CONTENTS

Access your FREE Book Bonuses
Enjoy Exclusive Content, Videos,
Thinking Tools, Community, Coaching
Opportunities, and More

VisionaryBook.com

FOREWORD BY GINO WICKMAN

Writing this foreword is an honor. I am all for anything that helps Visionaries. I am in awe of the many amazing resources to help Visionaries that have been created since the creation of the Visionary/Integrator concept over thirty years ago. Everything from Visionary forums, Integrator recruiters, fractional Integrators, the many resources at EOS Worldwide, and now this book.

It is hard to believe that it has been that long since I created the Visionary/Integrator concept. First, in the family business with my dad as the Visionary and me as the Integrator. I then taught the concept to my first fifty clients. I was a Visionary for twelve years, building EOS Worldwide with Don Tinney as my Integrator. I also put the teachings in my book *Traction*. The Visionary/Integrator concept, when implemented in an entrepreneurial organization, creates rocket fuel for the organization.

After years of proving the concept with thousands of entrepreneurs, it was time for a book to teach it in depth.

I still remember the first time I met Mark. I was teaching our "Boot Camp" for new EOS Implementers. He was seated immediately to my right. Even as one of the newest Implementers, Mark quickly became one of our best. He had early success with clients, broke a few records, and brought a level of energy and focus that was easy to notice.

When I put out a call for a coauthor to join me in writing a new book, one that would thoroughly teach the Visionary and Integrator concept, Mark threw his hat in the ring. I put him through a rigorous interview and evaluation process, along with a number of other candidates. It was critical to choose the right person for such an important project. In the end, Mark stood out. I chose him as my partner for what would become *Rocket Fuel*. And I'm glad I did.

When *Rocket Fuel* launched, we were both so proud of what we had created together. Soon, the book began to take on a life of its own. We've continued to work closely ever since, bringing this vital message to the world.

Since its release, *Rocket Fuel* has gone global, so far translated into five languages. It has introduced the world to the true power of the Visionary/Integrator Duo, and changed the way entrepreneurs talk about leadership. Hundreds of thousands of companies have applied its concepts. The language of Visionary and Integrator is now common, to the point that people use it for their tagline on social media.

Mark didn't just coauthor that book. He carried the torch forward. He created weekly YouTube videos to help Visionaries and Integrators learn and apply the concepts. He built a full online training academy, which EOS Worldwide now markets. He wrote blogs, taught workshops, keynoted conferences, and became a leader in our community of EOS Implementers. Over the years, I've watched him grow from that fresh new Implementer at Boot Camp into an expert on Visionaries and Integrators.

That growth and commitment are exactly why I'm writing this foreword. *Visionary* is the natural sequel to *Rocket Fuel*. *Rocket Fuel* gives you the V/I playbook, and this book gives Visionaries the added depth for their role.

Let me be clear. If you haven't read *Rocket Fuel*, start there. It's the foundation. It's essential. Then come back here. While *Visionary* builds on that foundation, most of the material in these pages is fresh and original. It is the culmination of Mark's years of experience working hands-on with Visionaries, and it goes deeper into their unique challenges and opportunities than ever before.

Rocket Fuel was, and is, a comprehensive guide for understanding and managing the Visionary/Integrator dynamic. It takes you from "Crystallizing" your understanding of the V/I structure to "Connecting" with your Integrator counterpart, and finally, "Maximizing" the power of the relationship. What this book does is take that work further. Mark zeroes in on the Visionary role and unpacks exactly what makes a Visionary great.

This is why I can say with conviction: this book is the essential sequel to *Rocket Fuel*. Every Visionary needs it. If you are sitting in the Visionary seat, you cannot afford to skip this book. It is not optional. It is your operating manual.

Mark has organized the path into Ten Pillars. If you embrace them, they will create freedom and maximize your impact. You will see yourself in these pages. Both the gifts and the challenges. You will find practical tools, frameworks, and stories that will guide you to become the kind of Visionary your company and the world desperately needs.

Mark takes the foundation we built together in *Rocket Fuel* and pushes it to a whole new level. He has distilled years of learning and teaching into a guide that will help you go further, faster. Without destroying yourself or your company in the process.

Visionary, this book is for you. I know what it's like to feel the frustration of being stuck in the weeds, pulled in too many directions, and worried that your company can't keep up with your ideas. I also know the exhilaration of living in your sweet spot. Seeing the future, sparking new ideas, and changing the world through your vision. The question is: which reality will you choose?

This book will show you the way. Read it carefully. Apply it faithfully. It will change the way you lead. And the way you live.

I trust Mark. I respect him. I consider him a dear friend. And I believe this book will unlock new levels of clarity, impact, and freedom for every Visionary who takes it seriously.

—Gino Wickman
Author of *Traction*, Creator of EOS,
and Co-Author of *Rocket Fuel*

VISIONARY—vi·sion·ary, *noun* \ ˈvi-zhə-ˌner-ē \,
First Known Use: 1702

: One who has clear ideas about what should hap-
  pen or be done in the future
: One who has a powerful imagination.
: One who sees visions.
: One who has unusual foresight.

Dreamer, Seer, Creator

INTRODUCTION

Without vision, the people perish.

—*Proverbs 29:18*

Sam slammed the car door, still clutching her security badge. Fired. Again.

Not for poor performance—her results were stellar. But she pushed too hard, moved too fast, and refused to stay in her lane.

Sam was genuinely "unemployable."

The career trail prior to launching her own company included multiple corporate scenarios where she'd been unable to steadily "color within the lines." Sometimes, the corporate bureaucracy couldn't handle her pushing for more. Other times, she couldn't handle them, repeatedly asking her to stop. They just kept telling her what to do—until she decided it was time to start telling herself what to do.

If this sounds familiar—you're not alone. You've probably been fighting against systems that were never built for someone like you. That tension you've always felt? There's a reason for it. And there's a way through it.

If you're a Visionary, you hate being told what to do. You have what I call a Free Streak[IP]. This isn't true of everyone. Some people don't mind being told what to do. They actually like it. That was a mind-boggling discovery for me! We're all different. And that's a good thing. Visionaries just happen to have a highly developed Free Streak.

Some Visionaries try to go it alone. Build a one-person empire. And for a rare few, that can work. But many of us are called to build something bigger. Something beyond us. And we can't do that solo.

WHAT IS A VISIONARY?

What is a Visionary? You are the future-oriented, idea-generating, external-facing engine of the business. As a Visionary, you are entrepreneurial, a creator, and likely a founder of your firm. Your vital counterpart in this role is an Integrator. They focus on the now. Driving execution and accountability from the inside. Together, you form a Visionary/Integrator (V/I) Duo—a truly powerful combination that can drive your business to the next level. You make it up, and the Integrator makes it happen.

There are some superpowers only a Visionary has. No one else can do these as well for the organization. As a result, these superpowers help define your role.

You See the Future First. Visionaries see the future—where things are headed. And based on that insight, where to best position the business to take full advantage of seeing it early.

You Spark the Fire. Visionaries are often the spark plug. The one in the organization that consistently gets us (and keeps us) thinking about that future, while the Integrator keeps us steadily moving forward in that direction.

You Live in Strategy, Not Execution. A visionary is great with R&D (more R than D) for new products and services, and always has a pulse on our market/industry. You think strategically, with the big picture in mind. You see the needs of clients in a way that others can't.

You Bring a Flood of Ideas. Visionaries generate lots of new ideas. We call this "twenty new ideas a week." Now, maybe eighteen of those ideas are not so great for us. In fact, one of those could potentially put us out of business. However, one of those ideas might be pure gold. It could take us to the moon! So we grab that one—and go execute.

You Stretch Reality. Visionaries sometimes create a "reality distortion field," a term used to describe Steve Jobs. It's a power that you unconsciously deploy when others are around you. You can get them to temporarily lower their assumptions about constraints. They think differently about what's actually possible. They temporarily join in your headspace and think, "Wow, maybe we could do that!" Once back on their own, they go back to thinking about all the reasons we can't do it. But now their thinking has been stretched—at least a little bit. And according to Ralph Waldo Emerson, "A mind, once stretched by an idea, can never return to its original size."

You're Obsessed with Learning. A Visionary is a learner. You enjoy discovering new stuff, learning about new stuff, and figuring stuff out. You'll dig in actively, hit a roadblock, and then study to find the answers.

You Solve the Right Kind of Problems. Visionaries creatively solve problems. Not the boring problems, but the really interesting, complex problems. The problems that need to be seen from an "outside the box" perspective.

You Handle the Big Relationships. Visionaries are great at big external relationships. In your industry. In the community. With your big, strategic customer or key vendor. You develop and nurture those big external relationships.

You Close. And finally, closing big deals. I really mean more closing than selling. A lot of times, the sales team can pretty much accomplish the job. Then we bring in our "big gun" Visionary at the end to get it over the finish line, right?

If most of the traits on this list describe you, you are a Visionary.

Of course, along with superpowers always come challenges. The fatal flaws of our hero. Those areas where you're just not as great, that don't feel natural to you. And some of these may sink you back down in your chair just a bit.

Visionaries often have difficulty being consistent. You go in this direction. And then you go in that direction. Inconsistency can create an effect we call "whiplash." The organization follows the gaze of the Visionary. Everybody's watching you. If you look in this direction, what does the whole organization do? They all look in the same direction with you. And what happens when you gaze in the other direction? Well, they start scrambling. Now half of them are starting to look the other way. Some are still looking in the first direction, and some are now looking right back at you! It creates this "whiplash," which creates friction in your organization. It drains a lot of energy. Think of that as energy "leakage." It's lost. You can't get that time and energy back once it's gone.

Visionaries tend to underdevelop their leaders and managers. This often happens because you keep jumping in and saving them. You don't let them grow because you have all the answers. And it's this "genius with a thousand helpers" mentality where, at the end of the day, everybody comes back to you. Because you're "the genius."

Another common challenge is "all gas pedal and no brake." You just go. You don't know how to slow down and get your momentum under control. And sometimes that can get you in trouble. You have "a Ferrari brain with bicycle brakes."

The last challenge I'll touch on is that your Visionary drive can be too intense for most people. You can "melt" people when they're trying to stand up to you. Or when they lean into you in some way. So you need people around you who are strong enough to lean back against your intensity, when appropriate, and not get melted. They also must be able to keep up with your pace. You run pretty fast. Can they hang with you without getting left behind?

THE INTEGRATOR

Your job as Visionary is to delegate the role of implementing your ideas to others in your company and elevate yourself to your true skill set. The work you were made to do. This will free up your creativity to grow the company.

Looking at the role of the Integrator, what is it that they do exactly?

They're the best person in your organization at leading, managing, and holding people accountable. They must set that bar super high and hold everybody to that standard.

They must be great at executing the business plan and delivering P&L results. All the departmental leadership roles come together at the Integrator. They're not just driving revenue. They're not just controlling the expenses. They're the ones bringing all that together, making sure that whatever spits out of the bottom line is what we want.

They integrate the major functions. They work harmoniously through and between all the different functions of the company to get us aligned and moving forward. On time.

They ensure we have great communication across the entire organization, making sure that all the circles stay connected.

They break the ties when necessary, making the call, so we don't get stuck or stay stuck.

Why is that their role? Well, they have superpowers too. Integrators are great at what they do—just like you're great at what you do.

Integrators are great at creating clarity.

They're great at resolution. You might leave a project without a tidy bow on it. You might not be as obsessed with getting the tidy bow on things. But they are. They can't have anything floating around loose.

Integrators are great at focus, accountability, and execution. You make it up. They make it happen.

They are the glue. They hold things together.

Integrators are consistent. They're beating the drum, creating a tempo for the organization.

They make sure that core processes are in place—and followed by all.

Now, just as we listed the Visionary's challenges, what are the Integrator's challenges?

First of all, it can often be a thankless job.

They are the "no" person. They have to say no—a lot. Sometimes they get accused of being pessimistic. Guess who accuses them of that? You do!

They do the dirty work. They fire people.

They don't get the same level of recognition that you do. And that's fine with them.

They're often accused of moving too slowly. Again, mostly by you.

Now you have a sense of both roles making up the V/I Duo. The two could not be more different. And their power lies in these differences. We call it polarity. Together, they combine their talents to create a powerful engine for business growth.

HOW WILL THIS BOOK HELP YOU?

This book is not just about the Visionary role—it's fundamentally about you, the human. You do not work in isolation. You are operating in an external environment that includes a relationship with your Integrator (and others).

Visionaries often get taken advantage of by people (and situations) in that external environment. You often put others (and the business) first—to your own loss. And, because of your position/power, you are uniquely vulnerable to certain external threats, which "normal" people usually don't have to worry about.

I need to speak to your internal self as well. That will then manifest in how you show up externally, which gives you a better chance of achieving what you really want and protecting you from the things you don't.

How is this book going to help you? I'll admit to feeling it poses a challenge for an excellent reason. I've basically written a how-to book for a group of people who hate being told what to do. Remember that Free Streak we talked about? How the hell is this going to work? Well, in the first place, everything in this book is presented as a choice for you. I'm not telling you what to do. If you want to do it, it must be your choice. Otherwise, it will never work.

Although I am an Expert EOS Implementer™, this book is not about EOS® (Entrepreneurial Operating System®), as introduced in Gino Wickman's classic book *Traction*. And it's not a rehash of *Rocket Fuel*. It's a playbook for you—the human being behind the role.

Over my many years of working with Visionaries, I have compiled a mountain of case experiences that have worked along with painful lessons from the cases that have not. Real-world stuff, not theory. My aim is to share a path lined with the tools that I've seen work best, so you can consider if they'll work for you.

That said, I'm sure there are other approaches that might also work. You choose. You decide.

And in the words made famous by Neil Peart: "If you choose not to decide, you still have made a choice."

There's only one objective for this book, and it could not be more simple. It's simply to make you *great*. To help you become truly *great* as a Visionary. You must get really clear on exactly what that means for you. Write it down.

From there, we've got some tools to help you figure out where you are now. And how to ultimately get to where you want to go. It's a never-ending journey.

WHY DO I LOVE ENTREPRENEURS?

To begin with, I can't count the number of times I've seen the following drama play out. Someone has an "entrepreneurial seizure." They see an opportunity and are compelled to pursue it. This will be their ticket to freedom! More money. More time. Meaningful impact. And all with their favorite people. They make "the leap," and the journey begins.

Now, fast-forward maybe twelve to twenty-four months. We drop back in and check on how they're doing. What do we see? Well, it's not pretty.

They've never worked more hours in their life. Somehow their 24/7 feels like 25/8!

They're hardly making any money. And if they did the math on the hours, they'd realize that this is the lowest-paying hourly job they've ever had.

They've made no real impact that they can see. Great opportunities keep floating past them. They're just too mired in the muck to make those moves.

And how about the people they're spending all this time with? Well, they don't exactly love them. In fact, they kinda feel stuck with them. Desperation breeds fear, and that fear drives them to hang on to the people who don't fit them. And to customers who don't need them. That's a poor formula for success.

You know, "stuck" is a pretty good word to describe this place. And it literally hurts my soul to see a courageous, well-intended entrepreneur find themselves stuck there. How can you not root for the person Teddy Roosevelt called, "The Man in the Arena?"

And yet it happens all too often. Most people never make it out of that darkness.

So this has become my life's calling. That's why I wrote this book. To help these courageous souls get unstuck. To help them get clear on where they really want to go. And to help them move in that direction. I enjoy nothing more than seeing an entrepreneur fight through that darkness and emerge on the other side. Their business begins to do for them what they wanted it to do in the first place. Their courage is rewarded. They win!

I love entrepreneurs. And I believe you are the answer to most of the important challenges we face on the planet (and beyond). I really mean that!

And I am one of you. As are most of my friends.

HOW DID I GET HERE?

By this point, you may be asking: Who is this guy? I'll begin by saying that I am a Visionary, but I did not always know it. I grew up in a small town in southeastern Oklahoma, then went off to the University of Oklahoma, "OU." After graduating, I joined a huge company called Procter & Gamble. That started me on what, I thought at the time, was gonna be a lifelong professional career path. I fully intended to be the CEO of P&G by the age of forty-three. I literally had it mapped out! Eventually, after first being told otherwise, I figured out that I needed a "top-tier" MBA to run P&G, so I entered business school at the University of Chicago.

In B-school, we'd regularly do team projects. I vividly remember one class called the "Strategy and Tactics of Pricing." A group would walk up in front of the class and present what their invented widget would do. "Here's how big the market is... Here's how much we can sell it for... It's gonna cost this much to make..."Then another team would explain that they'd found some unmet service need in the market. And they could deliver the service for this cost, and sell it for that price, and so on. As I watched one team presentation after another, I considered my day-to-day role at P&G: selling everyday household products to grocery stores. Then a realization hit me. What I was hearing from those teams in that class was giving me a lot more of a "charge" than what I was doing for P&G.

I had just caught the "entrepreneurial bug."

Looking back on it now, as a Visionary, I can see I was wired differently than most folks. My Free Streak was very strong. So I quit my job. I left a solid salary, great benefits, and a new promotion lying right on the table. I made what my friend Gino Wickman calls "the leap."

In hindsight, I probably should've told my wife before I did it. Hopefully, I'm a little smarter now. That move earned me more than a few gray hairs. I had to go break the news to her, which was really uncomfortable because she's not wired like me. She didn't realize that she somehow signed up for the "roller coaster thrill ride" when she married me.

So, she "got to" come along for this ride, as I began the process of starting the first of fifteen different companies (as of this writing) that I've either started up myself, bought from somebody, shut down completely, or sold off to somebody else. Some ventures worked out extremely well. I've made a hundred-fold cash-on-cash return in just a few years. And then, on the other end, I've lost my entire investment and then some.

As a founder and business operator, I learned some really important lessons. In particular, I learned the value of having an operating system for the business and for me. Then, over time, I shifted from being an operator to more of an advisory role and started to lead entrepreneurial peer groups. Members would ask me to help them implement an operating system in their organization. They kept twisting my arm, so I finally agreed to do it for one member. And I discovered something: Teaching folks how to implement an operating system was really fun for me! Knowing the impact that it would create for them, I loved seeing them begin the journey. I enjoyed helping them through the obstacles that they encountered along the way.

One day, I stumbled upon a webinar where Mike Paton was discussing EOS (the Entrepreneurial Operating System), as introduced in the book *Traction* by Gino Wickman. And it struck me as an even better approach than what I was using myself. Then I met Gino, the founder and creator of EOS, and became an EOS Implementer®.

Gino and I became fast friends. And ultimately, that led to us writing the book *Rocket Fuel* together. We joined forces and built on his invention. The experience of the Visionary/Integrator combinations in his world, combined with how I had experienced that same dynamic. *Rocket Fuel* detailed how the Visionary/Integrator structure could best work together to create a dynamic company. Along with how to get connected and maximize the relationship.

This book has its origins in that book. As we taught that material, I came to see the outlines of a program for Visionaries I called the "10 Pillars."

I introduced these 10 Pillars to the hundreds of Visionaries in attendance at a large conference, and they had a very positive response. It was the highest-rated session of the conference that year. So I built a course: The Visionary Masterclass.

We launched this program at an EOS Conference™ in San Diego. Based on the overwhelmingly positive feedback, we expanded and enhanced the program even more. We also developed a Visionary Report Card, which you'll see later.

This book is built from that training. It combines all the experience that went into developing it, plus the experience from those Visionaries who have come through it with us.

And that's where we are now. We're helping create the most powerful Visionary/Integrator Duos on the planet. This book is the next step in your journey to become a truly great Visionary—and maximize the power of your Visionary/Integrator Duo relationship. Let this be your guidebook. As you journey toward becoming truly great—as a Visionary.

WHAT TO EXPECT

Once we have discussed each pillar, you will find extra tools that will help you understand them. They are:

Transformation: At the end of every chapter, you'll find a thinking exercise. These questions will guide you to consider what you've learned. I've labeled these as "transformations" because they're designed to move you forward from where you are now and closer to where you want to go. Hopefully, you'll have some "Aha!" moments as you complete these reflections. They will show where you have gaps to work on, while highlighting areas where you already excel. The exercises aren't long. It's best to complete them immediately after reading the chapter, while the content is fresh. Consider the questions, make your notes, and commit to action. Then engage in the Community for even deeper learning.

Community: You'll have access to a Community just for book owners.

This is where you'll be able to bring your questions and discuss the transformation exercises with others who are also going through, or have gone through, their own transformation. Think of this as a peer group to help you anchor the learning. Peer groups are a proven force relating to entrepreneurial growth and development. How many of you are in a CEO peer group or something similar? This Community is another one of those, but for Visionaries who want to operate in a V/I Duo. That's pretty special! Be sure that you tap into that and take full advantage.

VisionaryBook.com

As you read this book, set your mind to own your experience. Engage in the material. Take full advantage of every opportunity laid out here. Write down anything that grabs you. All your notes will be great fuel and added motivation.

As you work your way through this book, collect your questions. As issues arise that are unclear, make a note. Then bring those questions to the Community.

Tools: Throughout the journey, I'll also introduce you to practical tools that have helped hundreds of Visionaries like you. Simple frameworks, exercises, and a powerful self-assessment will guide your growth. Plus, the private community is waiting to help you apply them.

These tools aren't just for reflection—they're for action. Don't worry, I'll walk you through each one as it shows up.

Now, I realize some of you may be brand new to *Rocket Fuel* or EOS teachings, while some may almost consider themselves experts. Most will fall somewhere in between the two. No matter where you are on that spectrum, you will learn things from this book. We talk a lot about the journey to mastery. It never ends.

If you're an expert, you've probably forgotten some stuff. Even experts, who've been doing this work for a very long time, forget things. An EOS "newbie" might post a question or comment in the Community, and you think, "You know what? I used to do that, and I've gotten away from it." You may need a reminder of foundational tools that you've drifted away from. You'll see familiar concepts, and now understand them in a new and different way because you've grown since you first learned them. And there's also much new material to learn. Expect all of that to happen for you as you go through this book.

To those who are newer on the journey, there are many "golden nuggets" scattered along the way. All to help make you a better Visionary. You must always be looking for them. You never know when they will pop up. Dan Sullivan, founder of Strategic Coach®, says, "Your eyes only see, and your ears only hear, that which your brain is looking for."

At the end of this journey lined with tools, you'll arrive at a place where the tools are a natural extension of you. Regularly using them to get clear, stay focused, and move ever closer to the unique freedom[IP] you want and deserve.

Sam didn't fix everything overnight. But once she stopped fighting who she was—and started building like a real Visionary—everything changed.

She's not doing it all herself anymore. And she's never going back.

You'll meet a lot more Sams in the pages ahead.

Some are still stuck. Some have broken through.

All of them have something to teach you.

Now it's your turn.

It's time to reclaim your energy. Focus your fire. And build with power. This is your chance to become truly great as a Visionary.

As my friend Justin Maust would say, "Let's freakin' go!"

THE 10 PILLARS OF VISIONARY GREATNESS

If you want to build a tall tower, you must first
spend a long time on the foundation.
—*Chinese Proverb*

This is your playbook for becoming a truly great
Visionary. Inside are the 10 Pillars—each one a powerful tool for unlocking your full potential. Think of the
10 Pillars as your journey of Visionary self-discovery.

Each pillar is numbered, and each contains wisdom for you, a key. Your job is to study it. Answer
the questions. Make a move. And—this is the hardest
part—commit to taking the first step. Most Visionaries
struggle here. Starting is easy—but committing? That's
what separates the wanderers from the greats.

Having completed one pillar, you advance to the next. In due time, you'll have unlocked the wisdom of all ten. You'll be armed with a new understanding of your Visionary self and the world in which you operate. The destination you seek will become more apparent, along with the actions required to get you moving in that direction with intent.

The journey starts with one powerful habit I learned from Stephen Covey: "Begin with the end in mind." So, "What does it look like to be truly great as a Visionary?" Your answer to that question becomes your "end in mind," at least for now.

Before you can build your future in the real world, you must build it in your mind.

Before you can build your future in the real world, you must build it in your mind. Every great Visionary starts here. The pillars will become a blueprint. You see what *could be*—not just what is. That's your superpower. But here's the catch: you have to *see it clearly* before you can *lead others* toward it. You have to hold the vision steady long enough for others to begin believing in it too. This mental construction is more than just a dream; it's a design. Like an architect creating renderings before the first stone is ever laid, you begin shaping your future with intention. Your clarity becomes contagious. Your team can't build what you haven't envisioned. So as you work your way through each Pillar, you're not just learning how to operate—you're assembling the mental framework of your future. The clearer it becomes inside you, the more unstoppable it becomes in the world. And here's the beautiful part. You won't be the same person when you finish this journey. The process changes you, shaping your thinking and sharpening your vision.

As you go through each Pillar, your perspective will evolve. You'll begin to think differently—about both the future and the present. You'll become more attuned to how you're doing right now—day to day. You'll begin to feel a gap between where you are and where you're meant to be. You'll feel overwhelmed. This is normal. Do not let it beat you down. Take hope in knowing that 80 percent will do it. You don't have to be perfect. If you can get 80 percent of the way there, you can become great. Every great Visionary has felt this creative tension and used it to shape their desired future.

This tension helps us too. In his classic *The Obstacle Is the Way*, Ryan Holliday channels the Roman emperor Marcus Aurelius, who said, "The impediment to action advances action. What stands in the way becomes the way." As we go through each Pillar, your gaps (or obstacles) in each area will become visible. Think of each gap you identify as a stepping stone to help you cross a river. This is your pathway: from where you are, perhaps frustrated and falling short, to where you want to be—truly great as a Visionary.

Your greatness is waiting. Let's go get it.

THE 10 PILLARS AT A GLANCE

Before we take a deep dive into each Pillar, allow me to introduce the overall framework. This will give you a high-level sense of how the whole program fits together.

1. Know Thyself	6. Think About What You Think About
2. Maintain Warrior Shape	7. Watch Out for Pitfalls
3. Surround Yourself	8. Help Others Stretch
4. Commit to Your OS	9. Go Slow to Go Fast
5. Support Your Integrator	10. Do No Harm

Pillar 1: Know Thyself

Great Visionaries start with the mirror. You've got to know you. Clearly understand your own wiring, motivations, and strengths. Then lean into what you do best and release the rest. Self-awareness fuels better decisions, stronger alignment, and greater impact. Tools like profiling assessments help you discover your true genius and align your focus with your Visionary role. Self-awareness ensures you clearly identify how things fit together, along with what energizes you, and what you should delegate.

Pillar 2: Maintain Warrior Shape

You can't lead at your best if you're running on empty. You'll need to be in warrior shape. Protect and strengthen your body, mind, and spirit so you can perform at a high level for the long haul. Healthy habits build the resilience and energy your role demands.

Pillar 3: Surround Yourself

Great Visionaries never go it alone. Surround yourself with people who complement your strengths, share your vision, and have your back. The right relationships form a powerful alliance that helps you go further, faster. Additionally, you'll benefit from the seven forces they collectively provide. Together, these people provide a strategic shield of support.

Pillar 4: Commit to Your Operating System

Freedom comes from structure. Fully commit to a proven way of operating. Your individual OS helps clarify what you really want in life. Your Visionary OS[IP] (the 10 Pillars) makes you great in this Visionary role. Your V/I Duo OS (the 5 Rules) maintains synergy and effectiveness in that vital relationship. Finally, your business OS (e.g., EOS) focuses the human energy in your organization. Full commitment in each maximizes your potential for achieving the vision and impact you seek.

Pillar 5: Support Your Integrator

Your Integrator turns your vision into reality. Protect and empower this partnership with clarity, respect, and trust. A healthy V/I relationship significantly amplifies your collective effectiveness. You will achieve more together than you ever could alone.

Pillar 6: Think About What You Think About

Your thoughts shape your reality. As a Visionary, the way you think drives the direction and health of your entire organization. Learn to notice your mental patterns, replace harmful ones, and focus on ideas that move you toward your vision. A disciplined mindset creates clarity, fuels creativity, and builds resilience in the face of challenges.

Pillar 7: Watch for Pitfalls

Even the best Visionaries can sabotage their own success if they're not paying attention. There are more than a few hazards along the path, and they'll bite you if you don't watch out for them. Visionaries must remain vigilant about common challenges like inconsistency, holding on to too much, or changing direction too fast. Recognize these pitfalls early, learn strategies to mitigate them, and maintain focus on steady progress. The more consistently you avoid these traps, the more positive energy and momentum you'll build.

Pillar 8: Help Others Stretch

There's a healthy way and an unhealthy way to stretch. Encouraging growth in your team members enhances collective performance, but you must do this thoughtfully. Push too little, and growth stalls. Push too hard, and people break. The right kind of stretch builds skill, confidence, and loyalty. Strengthen your team and your business for the long term.

Pillar 9: Go Slow to Go Fast

For most, if not all, Visionaries, slowing down feels wrong. Yet it's often the smartest move you can make. Pausing to think, clarify, and align prevents costly mistakes and confusion later. When you slow down on purpose, you create the conditions for real speed. The result is faster progress. Cleaner execution. And a team moving powerfully in the same direction.

Pillar 10: First, Do No Harm

Your actions as a leader carry weight. Sometimes more than you realize. A careless comment or hasty decision can cause damage that takes months to repair. Maintain awareness of unintended consequences, and regularly reflect on your leadership decisions. Leading with care builds trust, protects momentum, and strengthens the foundation for lasting success.

Let's kick things off with Pillar 1.

PILLAR 1

KNOW THYSELF

To know thyself is the beginning of wisdom.

—*Socrates*

Socrates said, "To know thyself is the beginning of wisdom." The shorter version, "Know thyself," was inscribed on one of the archos at the temple in Delphi. This was the place where the Oracle of Delphi, the priestess

Pythia, foretold her prophesies. You can see where the Greeks started when they searched for understanding. The idea of looking in the mirror is nothing new.

The Visionary role does not operate in isolation. You intersect with key relationships. You intersect with the marketplace and the community. You intersect with your specific business—not just the people, but the actual business. And if you're going to make these intersections work well for all involved, you start by taking a good, long look inside yourself. If you don't really understand who you are internally—where you're coming from and where you're going—these external relationships can start to swirl out of control. You'll begin to feel completely lost.

I'm going to walk you through an exploration to look at yourself and your world through a series of lenses. Each will add to your overall perspective and enable you to answer some essential questions that surround your Visionary role.

First, let's take a look at who you are, beginning with the typical traits we see in a Visionary:

- Sees the future and has a natural feel for where things are headed.
- Has lots of ideas; the "well" never seems to run dry.
- Thinks of many ideas at once.
- Enjoys solving BIG, interesting problems (and hates the boring ones).
- Is resilient and driven.
- Tolerates risk well.

- Is an entrepreneur (in the most classical sense of the word).
- Can't resist "taking the leap" to go make it happen; feels a powerful urge toward action.

These Visionary traits are broad, categorical, and describe a larger pattern. In working with thousands of Visionaries, we've learned that these descriptions ring true to them, within what we call the 80 percent rule. That rule reminds us that every single trait need not apply. If 80 percent rings true, the list is relevant to you. It fits.

However, just because you know you're in the Visionary bucket doesn't mean you know enough. Visionaries come in many flavors. You must dig deeper into your individual Visionary pattern to explore how you are naturally wired.

Fear not, there are tools that can assist you.

Your Wiring

Let's begin with some profiling tools that can really deepen your understanding.

The Crystallizer Assessment®. Start with the Rocket Fuel Crystallizer Assessment. Gino and I created this assessment to help you discover whether your unique leadership abilities align more closely as a Visionary or an Integrator. And sometimes the results will surprise you. If you haven't taken it yet, here's a link:

RocketFuelNow.com/Crystallizer-Assessment/

Additional Self-Awareness Tools. Once you know you're wired as a Visionary, it's time to get more granular. Several excellent tools can help you see more clearly how your specific Visionary strengths show up and how they interact with others.

Here are a few that we've found to be helpful:

- Kolbe A™ Index
- Culture Index™
- CliftonStrengths® (formerly Clifton StrengthsFinder®)
- The 6 Types of Working Genius®

Each of these is useful. However, I don't want you to think that there's any single one of them that is the end-all, be-all. Consider each one an additional data point in your journey toward self-discovery.

The Kolbe A Index is one of the twenty tools in the EOS Toolbox™—and is unlike any other assessment. The Kolbe A does not measure intelligence, personality, or social style. Instead, it measures your instinctive way of doing things, and the result is called your MO

(Method of Operation). It is the only validated assessment that measures a person's "conative" strengths. Getting directly to how people execute, as opposed to their IQ or personality.

Culture Index is another program that many of my private EOS clients have found valuable. It helps predict how we're intrinsically wired and how we're likely to interact with the wiring patterns of others. They have a framework of named "archetypes" for the significant profile patterns that exist in the world. This gives your team a shared language, which can also be very helpful.

CliftonStrengths (formerly Clifton StrengthsFinder®) helps you identify your top natural talents out of thirty-four possible themes. It's not about fixing weaknesses. It's about leaning into what you already do best. For Visionaries, this often highlights themes like ideation, strategy, and big-picture thinking. Once you know your strengths, you can shape your role around them and team up with others who fill your gaps.

The 6 Types of Working Genius is a newer model from Patrick Lencioni. It helps people discover their natural gifts in order to thrive in their work and life—they can better understand the types of work that bring them more energy and fulfillment. They avoid work that leads to frustration and failure. As a result, they can be more self-aware, productive, and successful. This is the only tool of its kind that is applied to work, so I encourage you to check it out.

While there are a ton of different profiling tools out there, the few that I've talked about can really help you to understand yourself—and your Visionary piece of the puzzle. I hope you see the power behind these assessments and set aside some time to complete a few.

VisionaryBook.com

You want to work on what you're naturally, truly great at. It's your gift, and everybody has one. It just takes a little work for you to identify it. Oddly enough, while it may not be obvious to you, those who work closely with you can easily see it. In fact, I strongly recommend asking a small circle of trusted people who know you well for their feedback on these questions: What am I best at? What's something you notice being easy for me that others struggle with? If you were going to describe my "superpower" to someone else, what would you say? Look for the patterns in the responses, and see what resonates with you.

Dan Sullivan created a concept that he calls Unique Ability®. It's the superpower that you were made for. It's almost effortless for you. It doesn't drain your energy. In fact, the more you do it, the more energized you become. It causes people to look at you and say, "Wow, how do you do that?" And you respond, "What? This is easy." That's when you realize it's actually not that easy for everybody else.

Daniel Pink's *Seven Smarter Questions* offer another powerful path of exploration. These prompts help uncover deep truths by looking at moments when you felt most alive, most appreciated, and most aligned. What fascinated you as a kid? When do you lose track of time? What do others thank you for? These questions point toward your natural genius—where passion and talent intersect. The process also looks forward, asking you to imagine life without money pressures and to consider what you'd regret not doing by the time you're ninety. This process helps you cut through the noise of today, bringing your true purpose and cause into focus, giving you a better sense of what actually drives you.

Now that you have a better sense of your wiring, it's time to explore your big "Why."

Your Why

Let's talk about your personal motivation. What drives you from the inside? What is propelling you from this place where you are now toward the place you want to end up? Have you thought about this deeply? At a level that's beyond money?

In *Start With Why*, Simon Sinek argues that successful leaders—and their organizations—are driven by a clear sense of purpose, or Why, which inspires others to follow. He emphasizes that people "don't buy what you do; they buy why you do it." As a Visionary, you must inspire others to buy into your vision.

Another model that has become popular of late is the Japanese concept of *ikigai*, your "reason for being." With ancient cultural roots, it represents the powerful intersection of what you love, what you're great at, what the world needs, and what you can be paid for. It's a holistic framework for purpose and fulfillment.

I should point out that your personal Why may well be different from the Why of your business. This is because some of you have more than one business, and each business has a somewhat different Why. While different, those business Whys should always be aligned with you.

Think about reviewing your company's vision and its unique purpose, cause, or passion (which answers the Why for that business), and the niche (which answers the What). You may feel like something's missing. You sit back and consider your whole world. Everything you want in life. You realize the Why + What combination for this business may not be *all* of you. Hopefully, it is completely aligned with you. However, it may just be one part of your world.

If you have multiple businesses, perhaps one is a vehicle for trying out new things as a "test bed." Another is driving a specific human impact that has deep meaning for you. Yet another is creating tremendous growth opportunities for the people in that organization.

Each contributes something toward what you want and moves in the direction of your personal vision. That is the umbrella under which everything must fall. If something doesn't fit, it's a distraction.

Therefore, you must become crystal clear on your own unique individual combination of motives that your business can serve in some way. This is how you avoid the "shiny stuff" that will distract you. The clearer you get on this, the better chance your company can help you achieve it.

To create this clarity, let's explore how each of these comes together in something I call your Intrinsic Genius[IP].

Intrinsic Genius

Intrinsic Genius is the unique intersection of what you're naturally great at, what you deeply love doing, and what intrinsically drives you. It's not just a strength or a passion; it's the powerful zone where your competence, joy, and drive converge to create your highest value and most fulfilling contribution. When you operate from your Intrinsic Genius, the place where these three elements converge, you experience flow, clarity, and energy. You unlock the kind of momentum that only comes from doing exactly what you were built to do.

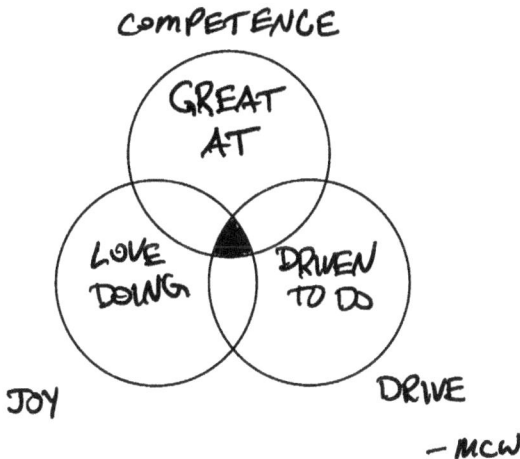

Here's the Intrinsic Genius Formula:

Intrinsic Genius = Competence × Joy × Drive

- **Competence** is what you're *naturally great at*—your innate talent or native ability that comes to you easily and produces extraordinary results.

- **Joy** is what you *genuinely love doing*—the work that lights you up, energizes you, and creates flow.

- **Drive** is the inner force that *propels you forward*—a synthesis of your **purpose** (why you exist) and your **cause** (what you're here to change).

When all three are present—talent, passion, and purpose-aligned motivation—you've found your **Intrinsic Genius.**

Discover Your Intrinsic Genius

While the outside sources I've listed are helpful to get you thinking, here is an exercise that zeroes in your focus. Take a few minutes to work through each step, and you'll find that the exercise will anchor the learning about yourself in a way that will make all the difference. This exercise will help you build your Intrinsic Genius. That is, it drills down to the heart of understanding your own personal combination of competence, joy, and drive.

Step 1: Focus on your Visionary seat. You're not here to do *everything*. You're here to do the few things only *you* can do. Write down all of your roles in your Visionary seat. For those who know EOS, where should those already be listed? Right. On the Accountability Chart®! To help you, I have provided your seat from the EOS

Accountability Chart below. If you are new to EOS, the Accountability Chart is simply an org chart on steroids. It strips away all those traditionally debilitating traps of hierarchy and titles. Instead, it will help you gain absolute clarity on exactly what each person is accountable for and the one person they are accountable to for those roles.

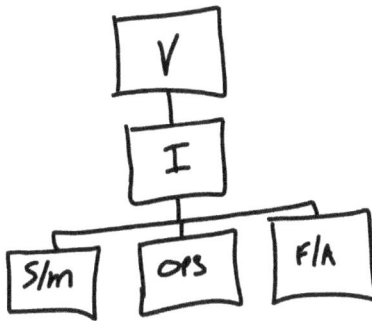

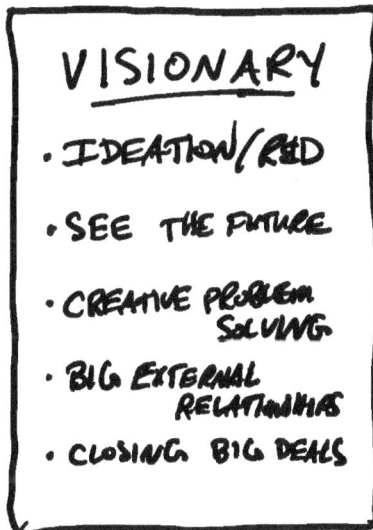

VISIONARY

- IDEATION/R&D
- SEE THE FUTURE
- CREATIVE PROBLEM SOLVING
- BIG EXTERNAL RELATIONSHIPS
- CLOSING BIG DEALS

To fill out your seat on the Accountability Chart for the Visionary function, ask yourself: What do you want to do most, the thing that only you can do for the business? Write them down. Keep these roles clearly in mind as you move through the rest of the exercise.

The goal here, simply put, is to focus time and energy on your Intrinsic Genius—that place where your competence, joy, and drive intersect.

Step 2: Activity Brain Dump. Ask yourself: *What are all the things you currently spend time and energy on as a Visionary?*

Now that you've captured your roles, we're going to brain dump your activity list. I want you to do a dump. Do not sit back and think; just lean forward and write.

These are the things that you do. They consume your time and energy. Think of your activities during a day, a week, a month. Think across whatever time spans you typically consider. What's taking up your time and energy right now? The trick is to get those ideas that are top of mind out on paper. Let it flow. Then you can stop and consider them. Include everything. Big or small. Recurring or not.

Step 3: Plot on the Joy/Competence Matrix[IP]. Some of you may already be familiar with this step. It was inspired by an EOS tool called Delegate and Elevate®. I'll quickly set up how it works. Take the "brain dump" list you just completed. You're going to map each entry into the Joy/Competence Matrix quadrants illustrated on the chart below. To allow plenty of space, divide a piece of paper into 4 quadrants as shown.

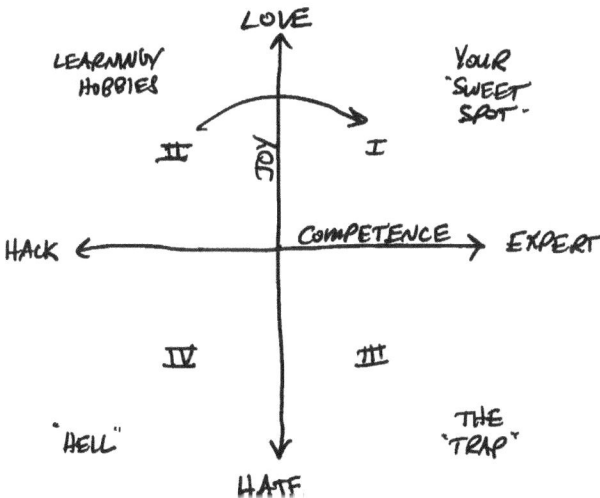

—mcw

Here's how the quadrants work. The top quadrants are for activities that you enjoy. The bottom quadrants are for those you don't. So you can think of the vertical as the *joy* axis, where the top is joy—"I love this stuff"—and the bottom is the stuff you really hate. The horizontal axis is basically your level of *competence*. On the left are the things you're not good at. On the right, put the things that you're good at, or maybe even great. Pretty simple, right?

Let's dive into each quadrant to help you really master this step.

Quadrant I: Love it + Great at it. This is your sweet spot. This is where you want to live. You can do things here that nobody else can. Your energy continuously grows and expands, which multiplies your impact. One unit of time/energy spent here generates a disproportionate return. This is where you can truly change the world. If you let other activities take you out of this quadrant, you're doing the world a disservice.

Quadrant II: Love it + Not Great at it. This is where I often see learning and hobbies emerge. You're drawn toward these activities for some reason. Maybe you haven't fully developed your capabilities here, but you're happy to keep working at it. Because of this passion, you will improve. Sometimes items in this quadrant make the transition over into Quadrant I, as your competence eventually improves to become Great.

Quadrant III: Hate it + Good/Great at it. I think about this one as the "Trap." Chris Jones, a fellow Expert EOS Implementer, calls it the "Suck Bucket." Guess who wants you to spend time here? Everybody else! Why? Because you're so darn good at this stuff. You make it look easy. But you hate it. Working at it sucks the life out of you. You may have developed this capability out of pure necessity as you fought for the survival of your business in the early days. Whatever the original reason, you got really good at it, but it simply does not bring you joy. As a result, time spent here not only consumes your time, but it also consumes a disproportionate share of your energy. And once those energy units are burned, they're gone. They are no longer available for you to invest in a high-return area, such as Quadrant I. You must work intentionally to get yourself out of this quadrant ASAP.

Quadrant IV: Hate it + Stink at it. This one seems obvious. I call it "hell." Nobody in their right mind should be choosing to spend time and energy here. And yet, when I take Visionaries through this exercise, far too many report spending a non-trivial percent of their time in this quadrant. What's worse is when I expand the question to ask, "How much time would you like to spend in each quadrant?" Some people still actually choose to spend a portion of their time in this one! I hope that's not you.

See this quadrant for what it is—*hell*—and solve for it above all else. Life is too short. Think of this one as a black hole—that nothing good ever escapes from again. It consumes your energy, your time, and it comes at a great expense to the business.

However, here's a secret about Quadrant IV. Those things that you hate? Somebody else will list those as activities they love! This may shock you, but it is absolutely true. And it's a powerful truth to realize. Maybe you thought you were doing the world a favor by taking on all that suffering, while, in reality, you were keeping someone else from a chance to operate in their sweet spot. Your quadrant IV object of hate might be their quadrant I sweet spot. So consider that as you list all the possibilities for delegation.

Now take everything you wrote on your "brain dump" list, and put each in the appropriate quadrant on your page. As you do this, reflect on what you see: What's the pattern? What's common about these activities?

It's time for us to explore these patterns. Grab another clean sheet of paper for this step, and draw a vertical line down the middle, creating two columns. Over the left column, write Joy, and write Competence over the right.

Studying your quadrants, remember that the two axes were *joy* and *competence*. First, notice those items that fell "above the line" for you are in the top two quadrants. These activities bring you joy. Think about what you are really passionate about. What patterns can you detect in them? Write these in the Joy column. Just let it flow. Capture what you notice. Then go back through and see if you can cluster some of them: certain types of creative tasks, strategic sessions, brainstorming new ideas, or key external meetings.

Then, look for what you're really great at, on the right side of the *competence* axis. These activities reflect your talents. Your natural strengths. List those in the Competence column. Again, look for the pattern.

Next, try to distill all of the entries down into the common elements that you see in your Love/Great quadrant—the quadrant of the stuff where you're truly great and that you truly love. Quadrant I. Your sweet spot. Can you distill that down to just a few words or a sentence? Write it down.

Mine is "LCD," which stands for *Learn. Create. Deliver.* These are the types of activities that clearly fall in my sweet spot: gathering and synthesizing new information from a variety of sources, taking what I've learned and converting it into teaching content, frameworks, tools, books, and courses, and then delivering that content live or via recordings. Any time I'm doing activities other than this, I know I have a new issue to solve: "How do I get back into LCD?"

Step 4: Explore Your Drive. The third component of your Intrinsic Genius is Drive—the inner force that propels you forward, connected to a meaningful external impact. Drive, in this context, is simply a synthesis of your Purpose and your Cause. This really begins to get to the heart of your individual Why and the impact you want to have on the world.

Now let's explore these patterns. Grab one more clean sheet of paper for this step, and draw a vertical line down the middle, creating two columns. Over the left column, write Purpose, and write Cause over the right.

Beginning with Purpose, think deeply about the following questions, and capture your thoughts in the left column:

- *Why do you exist?*
- *What's the deeper meaning beyond making money?*
- *What are you here to do beyond business or success?*
- *If you could only be remembered for one contribution, what would it be?*
- *What gives your work a deeper Why?*

Your Why is the big dent that you personally want to make in the universe—a goal that deeply resonates with you. It's the reason you were put on the planet. You're drawn toward it, and it drives you to get up and take action in that direction every day. Write it down.

Moving ahead to Cause, give similar thought to these questions as well, adding your thoughts to the column on the right:

- *Is there a movement, mission, or injustice you're working to advance or fix?*
- *What frustrates or energizes you most about the world, your industry, or your clients?*
- *What do you want to change, challenge, or elevate in the world?*
- *Who are you driven to help, and what are you helping them unlock?*

As you look over the thoughts you've captured, try to distill the essence of each column. How would you simply state the pattern you see for Purpose? And for Cause? How would you bring those two together? Write it down.

For me, this element is all about helping entrepreneurs. I believe that's why I'm here. And I'm driven to help them overcome many of the frustrations I've encountered through my own entrepreneurial journey. It's simply the stuff I needed myself.

Step 5: Craft Your Intrinsic Genius Statement. We have one big question left to answer: What is *your* Intrinsic Genius?

Let's pull together all the work you've done so far with an example.

Here is my personal example:

- **Competence:** I create tools that help people think. (Create.)
- **Joy:** I'm a student, a teacher, and a coach. (Learn. Deliver.)
- **Drive:** I help driven, visionary entrepreneurs get unstuck, to discover and expand their unique freedom exponentially.

That's very meaningful to me. I care deeply about entrepreneurs—particularly the Visionaries. I consider this group my tribe. I get them, and they get me. And I also deeply believe that this group—and their ability to truly impact the world—is the key to solving most of the major problems we're facing today.

Now it's your turn:

- What's your Competence?
- What's your Joy?
- What's your Drive?
- Write them down and anchor them in your mind.

YOUR INTRINSIC GENIUS:

Competence (Great At): _____

Joy (Love Doing): _____

Drive (Propels You Forward): _____

If you can, bring the three together into a single sentence or short paragraph that captures the impact you are Driven to create, through your Competencies (Great At), that bring you Joy (Love Doing).

Again, here's my personal example:

"I'm a student, a teacher, and a coach. I create tools that help people think, so that I can help driven visionary entrepreneurs get unstuck, to discover and expand their unique freedom exponentially. I make the world better through them."

This is not a marketing slogan. The intent is purely to create clarity for you. Don't get caught up in "marketing-ese," and try to make it "slick." In some ways, the clunkier the better. As long as it creates clarity for you.

Pro Tip: Consider getting some feedback from people who know you well. People who are close to you can see certain qualities about you much more clearly than you can. It's obvious to them. Maybe you're part of a peer group where you've developed a deep level of trust, and you can count on them to always speak truth to you. Especially when you need it. All that said, you are the ultimate judge. Take the input of others as data points, and run them through your own filter. In the end, you must decide. And when you get it right, you'll know it.

The right answer here will truly fit you. It's your starting point. Come back to it often. Let it evolve until it truly becomes a keystone for you.

You know you have Visionary DNA. The profiling tools have helped you see more clearly how you're wired. Your Intrinsic Genius has helped you see what drives you from your core. So now we turn our lens toward the reality of your current situation and the things around you that you'd love to see changed. And the sooner, the better. Let me introduce you to the perfect tool for that. It's called the "Wish List."

Wish List

The wish list originally came from one of Gino's clients, Michael Morse. Michael did a massive brain dump as he thought through issues like:

- If I had a great Integrator here, what problems would go away?
- What would we finally be able to get done?
- What could I get off my plate so I don't have to deal with it?

    As you read through Michael's Wish List, which items strike a chord for you?

	Michael Morse's Actual Integrator Wish List
1	Be the quarterback for the move back to Southfield, including phones, computers, boxes, and furniture.
2	Review Insurance policies. Meet with agents. Compare prices and companies and coverages: workers' compensation, business, home, lake house, malpractice, and employee liability policy.
3	Help analyze and help implement the East Side office if it is a go.
4	Analyze numbers for each person. Help put a number on each person. Help us set proper goals for the coming year.
5	Set up and implement an employee review system. Make sure it gets done and done right.

6	Help us come up with better bonus and compensation systems.
7	Go through and review all employee files to make sure they all have proper documentation signed and in the file. Make sure all attorneys have signed contracts. Make sure they cover everything.
8	Get a handle on how we close files. Want to do it all on disk and get rid of storage costs. Get a handle on what storage company has and when we can start purging old documents to save money. Possibly purge half of what we have there, as we pay per box.
9	Make sure phones are being answered quickly and promptly. If not, figure out why.
10	Make sure all Core Values are being lived by all. Brainstorm and set up ways for the Core Values to become part of everyone's daily lives at the firm.
11	Make sure all 90-Day Priorities are being done, and help people who are having a hard time getting them done.
12	Be my eyes on the books so I don't have to. Review bank statements. Watch the money in the account daily or weekly.
13	Review the vendor list and start getting a handle on all payables, and start negotiating and looking for alternatives. Example: copy services, postage, subpoena services, running/filing services, etc.
14	Review and perfect the new employee time procedure.
15	Get a handle on what could make secretaries more efficient and happier.
16	Make sure everyone is working to capacity, no slackers.
17	Make sure the office is as paperless as possible.
18	Interview and compare several Time Matters people and hire a new person in the office. Get Time Matters working as to make us more efficient.

19	Organize Word system so it's easy. Probably will need different software for that purpose.
20	Make sure clients are being called and informed about their pending cases. Follow up on it. Pull files and see if this is being done. Make sure lawyers are putting proper notes in files.
21	Get a good handle on lawyer teams and make sure they're running smoothly. Get a handle on the capacity of each person.
22	Help us cut costs.
23	Come up with, manage, and organize quarterly events for team building.
24	Review and negotiate all contracts, including advertising.
25	Look for missed opportunities for getting new business. Review what is and is not working.
26	Be my eyes and ears when I am not there or when the rest of the executive team is not there.
27	Be in charge of all scorecards, blue sheets, and gathering financial information. Interact with our lawyers and CPAs when needed.
28	Eventually run our quarterly meetings.
29	Make sure we roll out what and when we need to roll out.
30	Interview and make sure tech people and web people are the best we can get for the money.
31	Monitor what other employees are doing on their systems via monitoring software that has been bought and implemented.
32	Manage each team. Go to each team meeting. Make sure of good follow-through. Make sure team meetings and the team itself run smoothly.

Michael Morse, Founder of the Mike Morse Law Firm, is a pure Visionary in every sense. You can learn more about his V/I story on page 56 of *Rocket Fuel*.

So Michael just dumps this wishlist out of his brain, and then sits with his Integrator and says, "All right, here's my wish list. What can you do for me?"

He then works collaboratively with the Integrator to compartmentalize these things in a way that allows them to chip away at the wish list over time.

Some of these goals you won't accomplish right away because a more important issue is on the front burner. What you want the Integrator to handle has to be placed in the proper "compartment":

- Is it a big focus for this year that becomes a one-year goal?
- Is it a key initiative (in EOS terms, a Rock) to focus on this quarter?
- Is it a long-term issue, beyond 90 days in the future?
- Is it a short-term issue (less than 90 days) that we'll need to engage this quarter?
- Is it simply a to-do that we can knock out this week?

A common fear Visionaries share is that their great idea will be lost. Putting items in their proper buckets, or compartmentalizing, helps you see that nothing is getting lost. All your valuable ideas are actually going somewhere, even if they're slated for later. This can't happen unless you take the time to generate your Wish List. It all starts there. Then you can get aligned with your Integrator. The two of you can get on the same page about what's really important to you,and then decide in which order you will make them happen. Together.

Now you must ask yourself the key Wish List question:

"What do I wish we could get done, take off my plate, or simply make go away so I don't have to deal with it anymore?"

These are the jobs that drive you crazy. They suck the energy out of your life. You've probably been wrestling with them for years and have not been able to figure out a way to break through. So sit down and make your Wish List. Then discuss it with your Integrator.

At this point, you've explored yourself and the landscape around you. You clearly see what needs to change. Now it's time to take that understanding and begin solving a vital puzzle.

The Two-Piece Puzzle

While "knowing thyself" directly impacts you—the Visionary—it also shapes what you ultimately need in an Integrator. In *Rocket Fuel*, Gino and I introduced the idea of the Two-Piece Puzzle. It describes how you (the Visionary) fit together with your Integrator.

We've all wrestled with trying to force together two puzzle pieces that didn't really fit, even if they were very close. The pieces either fit, or they don't. Solving this puzzle requires discovering and defining the "shape" of those two connecting edges. Where the Visionary piece connects to the Integrator piece. If you can clearly see the shape of your Visionary edge, the complementary Integrator edge will emerge.

Defining your edge comes from all the work you've just completed. You now see your Visionary DNA. You know your Crystallizer results. You've drawn patterns from various profiling tools. You defined your Intrinsic Genius. And you know what's on your wish list. All of this combines to inform your shape and the complementary shape of the Integrator edge that will fit with you. If you don't understand your Visionary self, you can never really understand the complementary Integrator shape that you seek.

Duo Fit describes how these two Visionary and the Integrator pieces fit together. We're looking for a combination that is complementary. It shouldn't have a ton of overlap, where both of you are strong in the same things. When we both instinctively gravitate to the same area of responsibility, we end up fighting for the wheel and getting in each other's way.

We're looking for a V/I combination where the coverage of leadership strengths is complete. We also don't want to have a bunch of gaps where neither is strong. Instead, we fill each other's gaps. Fitting neatly together, like a two-piece puzzle. For more on Gap and Overlap, see our Resource page:

VisionaryBook.com

Defining your Visionary edge in this way enables you to seek and find your complementary Integrator edge. When done well, these two pieces click together perfectly. How's your Duo Fit? When you look at how your Integrator fits with you, can you hear that solid "click"?

As I taught this concept more and more, it became apparent that there was another essential element, which was a natural extension of our model—a third piece And so, the Three-Piece Puzzle was created.

The Three-Piece Puzzle

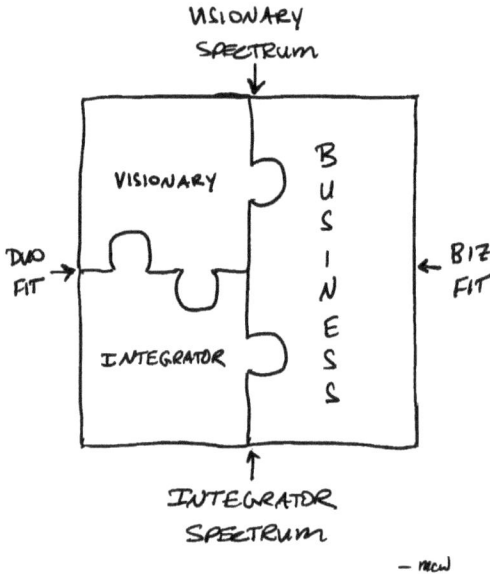

In this expanded model, we see that we must also consider the Business Fit. This gives us two additional edges to solve for:

1. where the Visionary piece fits with the business, and
2. where the Integrator piece fits together with the business.

Every business has a different situation in terms of what they really need in a Visionary—and what they really need in an Integrator—and these needs both fall somewhere along a spectrum, which is driven by the business. There's one for the Visionary and a second for the Integrator. These two spectrums help us understand the range of what the business might need from these two roles. We'll begin with the Visionary piece of the puzzle first, and the Visionary Spectrum we introduced in *Rocket Fuel*.

The Visionary Spectrum

How much Visionary energy does your business really need? And how much do you naturally have to offer?

From the perspective of the business, we must consider three major factors:

1. **Industry Type:** Different industries have different demands for Visionary leadership.

2. **Growth Aspirations:** Your business's growth expectations play a crucial role. Higher growth targets demand a more Visionary approach.

3. **Degree of Market Change/Complexity:** Market dynamics, competition, and complexity levels compound the need for Visionary leadership.

At one end of the spectrum, a business may need a "pioneer" like a Steve Jobs, an Elon Musk, or a Palmer Luckey—someone we might consider to be really "out there" as a Visionary. Each of these individuals has dealt with tremendous complexity, rapidly changing technology, and super-long planning horizons that extend well beyond this decade. Global supply chains. Regulatory uncertainty. Fierce competitive pressure.

A business on the other end of the spectrum doesn't move like that. It's almost the opposite of the above examples. There isn't much complexity. Relevant technology is pretty stable. Plans rarely look beyond this year. The supply chain is diverse and readily available. Regulatory pressure is minimal, and demand is either in equilibrium with supply or there's even more demand than you can fill. This market isn't changing very fast. And that's okay. That sort of business doesn't need as much Visionary energy. Skilled trades sometimes fall into this category: plumbing, electrical, HVAC, drywall hanging—you get the idea. On this end, we might jokingly say that a "Minimal" Mr. Magoo visionary would do. (For younger readers, Mr. Magoo was a classic cartoon character from the 1950s, with extreme nearsightedness, which he stubbornly refused to admit.)

So, on one end, you'll need a Pioneer type who can see w-a-a-ay out there. On the other end, you'll only need a Minimal-type, like Mr. Magoo, who doesn't need to see much of the future. In my experience, the Minimal scenario is pretty rare. Less than 10 percent of businesses. Consider the skilled trade industry examples provided above. The ones I've encountered often have aggressive growth aspirations, and they are strong innovators. In some cases, I'd consider those businesses to be Pioneers in their industry. So, if that's what you want, you will naturally need more Visionary energy. Yet if you truly are in a simple industry, with simple market dynamics, and minimal growth aspirations, then Minimal may be right for you. In fact, in that business, you might even be able to simply eliminate the Visionary seat by distributing its function across other members of the leadership team. No V/I Duo at the helm, just an Integrator. If that is your situation, this book is not for you.

Think about the range of the Visionary spectrum. Both ends are still generating ideas and thinking about the future—just at different levels.

Minimal Visionary: Focused primarily on day-to-day operations.

> **Industry Type**: Low complexity, slow-moving, stable
> **Growth Aspirations**: Minimal annual growth expectations
> **Market Change/Complexity**: Stable, minimal change

Basic Visionary: Some Visionary input is needed. Requires some forward-thinking to navigate changes.

> **Industry Type**: Low to moderate complexity, some changes
> **Growth Aspirations**: Moderate growth expectations
> **Market Change/Complexity**: Moderate competition and change

Balanced Visionary: Requires balancing between innovation and operational efficiency, managing both the present and the future.

Industry Type: Moderate complexity, with regular change ongoing
Growth Aspirations: Mixed growth expectations (some low, some high)
Market Change/Complexity: Dynamic market with occasional challenges

Strong Visionary: Requires intense Visionary leadership that is vital for innovation and navigating complex challenges.
Industry Type: High complexity, rapid changes.
Growth Aspirations: High annual growth expectations
Market Change/Complexity: Constantly evolving, highly competitive

Pioneer Visionary: Requires Visionary leaders who push the boundaries of innovation in a rapidly changing landscape. These Visionaries are the true pioneers.
Industry Type: Cutting-edge, high-tech industry, extreme complexity
Growth Aspirations: Extremely high annual growth expectations
Market Change/Complexity: Frequent and disruptive changes

Understanding the Visionary Spectrum is essential for making informed decisions about top-level leadership and strategy for your organization. By honestly and accurately assessing the needs of your business, you can ensure that you have the right level of Visionary energy to drive success.

As you examine the illustration in more detail, remember that all businesses, and all Visionaries, fall somewhere along that spectrum, including you. Now let's plot where both you and your business fall.

Ask yourself: Where do my capabilities fall on the spectrum? Let me make an important note here. As I ask you questions throughout this book, I urge you to be as honest as you possibly can. That is what will help you the most. Pretending to be someone you're not will simply mask reality and lead you down a foolish path. The fact is, the truth will eventually reveal itself, sometimes painfully. If you were not completely honest, you would have lost all that time in between, when you could have been moving forward.

Go ahead and mark a "V" on the illustration for where you see yourself. Be very honest. Wherever you fall, there's no judgment. All Visionaries have their role. And every business has a certain level of need for this Visionary energy.

Now let's answer the related question about your specific business: How much Visionary does your business actually need? Again, be really honest. Place a "B" in that place on the spectrum.

Sit back and examine the relationship between where you fall on the spectrum (V) and where your business falls (B). Perhaps you discover there is an appropriate level of fit between you (as a Visionary) and your Business. The Business's need for Visionary (VIS) energy falls relatively close to where you fall on that spectrum—indicating the level of VIS energy you're naturally inclined to bring. This would validate that we're starting in the right place. You likely feel very good about what you bring to this Business and the opportunity it provides for you.

However, in some cases, this is not what you find. Instead, you find there is a significant gap between where your V and your B fall on this spectrum. Maybe you see that the Business actually needs more Visionary energy than you naturally bring. On the other hand, maybe you bring much more than it needs. In either case, this likely does not surprise you. It simply clarifies a feeling that you already had.

V > B: "This Business is holding me back."

B > V: "Am I holding this Business back?"

If your V is greater than the B, you're likely bored at some level. As a result, you start looking to "scratch the itch" in different ways. This often leads Visionaries to begin exploring/starting lots of other things that are well beyond the "Core Focus" of their particular Business. This Visionary often feels they are missing an X factor. And they're uncertain that this particular Business will ever be able to deliver it.

As a reminder, Core Focus is an EOS term that answers the questions Why and What for your business. We must be clear on what motivates us to get up and go every day and having it resonate throughout the organization. With that, we're also crystal clear on what business we are actually in, what we fundamentally do.

For example, consider one of my client company's Purpose: Saving Lives. Their Niche: mobile medical diagnostics. Such clarity helps you, as Visionary, avoid chasing shiny objects. It becomes a powerful filter for you and the team to hold new ideas up against, and to evaluate whether they actually could help us make progress in that direction.

On the other hand, if your B is greater than your V, you're likely frustrated by what others want you to do. They see possibilities that aren't obvious—or attractive—to you. And they push you to pursue them. Maybe your other Owners see/want more, or maybe you have some members of your leadership team who have a Visionary horizon beyond your own.

More than once, I've seen a V/I Duo end up swapping roles as they better understood the needs of the business. On a recent episode of the *Rocket Fuel Podcast*, Jonathan Reynolds and Scott Seefeld shared their story with me. Scott hired Jonathan to set up a new recruiting division for his accounting firm, Titus. As the project evolved, Scott realized their roles needed to shift. At this stage, the recruiting business was more dynamic than the accounting side. And Jonathan was demonstrating a strong ability toward the higher end of the Visionary Spectrum. In this case, Jonathan was actually better wired to serve as the Visionary, while Scott, the CEO, was better suited as the Integrator.

While this does happen, it's very rare. And, when it works, there is 100 percent alignment between the two. Along with a great deal of appreciation for the Intrinsic Genius that each one brings to the combination. The most important note here is that we solve for making sure that your level of Visionary energy is a good fit for this specific business. If not, you will be frustrated, and the business will suffer.

Either way, it's critical that we get alignment on where we're headed. A single ship can't sail toward opposite ports.

The Integrator Spectrum

Every Visionary and every business needs an Integrator who can address their specific needs. We visualize these varying degrees of Integrator energy falling along an Integrator spectrum. As with the Visionary Spectrum, multiple factors converge to explain this range. Industry type, organizational growth, market complexity, and speed of change all impact how much Integrator our business needs.

OPERATIONAL INTEGRATOR

ORGANIZATIONAL DEVELOPMENT INTEGRATOR

THOUGHT PARTNER INTEGRATOR

INTEGRATOR SPECTRUM

PEOPLE DEVELOPMENT INTEGRATOR

STRATEGIC INTEGRATOR

Operational Integrator: Focused on managing people, processes, and data with shorter time frames. More tactical, functional projects.

>   **Industry Type**: Mature, stable markets. Focus on operational efficiency and incremental improvements
>   **Growth Aspirations**: Steady, moderate growth. Focus on cost control and process optimization
>   **Market Change/Complexity**: Low complexity, stable market conditions. Focus on maintaining and improving existing operations

People Development Integrator: Mentors and develops the skills of others by gaining an understanding of roles outside their own.

Industry Type: Reliant upon skilled talent development and nurturing
Growth Aspirations: Moderate growth. Strong emphasis on talent acquisition, innovation, and learning
Market Change/Complexity: Increasing complexity as talent and skill development become paramount. Adapts to rapidly changing markets and technologies

Organizational Development Integrator: Specializes in creating a cohesive and efficient organization, ensuring the right people and structure.
    Industry Type: Frequent structural changes. Need for agile responses
    Growth Aspirations: Experiencing restructure, expansion, or cultural shifts
    Market Change/Complexity: Highly complex, constant change. Requires aligning structures, processes, and people

Strategic Integrator: Develops market trends, product relevance, and service offerings strategies. Breaks Visionary's big ideas down into executable strategies.
    Industry Type: Innovative and dynamic industries. Crucial to stay ahead of market trends
    Growth Aspirations: Focused on rapid growth, product development, and market expansion
    Market Change/Complexity: Complex. Adapting quickly to evolving trends and technologies

Thought Partner Integrator: Serves as the Visionary's thought partner with a long term view. Focusing on complex, mission-critical impacts in a constantly changing environment.

Industry Type: Characterized by disruptive innovation, global reach, and complex ecosystems

Growth Aspirations: Substantial, often global growth. Influenced by external geopolitical factors and technology shifts

Market Change/Complexity: Highly complex enterprise-wide impacts

Some Integrators can handle a great deal of complexity, while others cannot.

On the "Operational" Integrator end of the spectrum, the Integrator is more like a project manager. They're outlining the details, laying out the plan, and keeping things moving forward.

Contrast this with somebody who's on more of the "Thought Partner" end of the spectrum. They are comfortable dealing with tons of complexity. Maybe we've got all different kinds of offerings in the market. Maybe we're in many different markets. Maybe we're global, and we have different kinds of regulatory environments. Maybe we have lots and lots of people.

All those factors create different levels of complexity that your Integrator must be able to manage consistently at a high level of performance. The best Integrators adapt and grow, supporting their Visionary while meeting organizational needs.

So again, we ask the important question about your business: How much Integrator does this business actually need?

Place a "B" in that place on the spectrum. That's one side of the shape of our Integrator piece.

Now that you have determined where your Integrator fits on their Spectrum, let's return to the idea of a Duo Fit and how these puzzle pieces all fit together. When you look at the Three-Piece Puzzle illustration, I want you to imagine that you're backing into the shape of the Integrator piece.

You must understand the shape of your Visionary edge—where you match up with the Integrator, which also gives you the Integrator's corresponding edge. And you must understand where your Business falls on the Integrator spectrum. This gives you the shape of the edge where the Integrator matches up with the business. Imagine drawing those shapes based on the information you now have on each of those edges.

Well, what do you know? If we can see the shapes of two pieces (Visionary and Business) in our three-piece puzzle, that actually tells us the shape of the missing Integrator piece. Once you know the shape of the missing Integrator, you have a much better chance of going out into the world and finding the right one.

1. First, we must know ourselves on multiple levels. We must look inside.

2. Next, we must know our business and what it needs.

3. From there, we can begin to know our Integrator. The other side of our V/I Duo.

Once you know your shape and the shape of your missing Integrator piece, you will be able to go out and find them, solving the Three-Piece Puzzle for your Business. When all three edges "click" together solidly, the power of Rocket Fuel will happen.

Transformation

To wrap up this Pillar, you're going to use a tool I mentioned in the Introduction: the Visionary Report Card.

Visionary Report Card

- Check each sub-area where your Visionary is consistently achieving success.
- Rate each major area on a scale of 1-10 (10 being best).

Pillars	Mindsets		1-10
1. Know Thyself	Profile results identified (Kolbe, Culture Index, Working Genius, etc.) and using them to guide decision-making and alignment.	☐	
	Intrinsic Genius* (personal combination of competence, joy, and drive) defined.	☐	
	Joy/Competence Matrix* done regularly, enabling Visionary to stay in their "sweet spot."	☐	
	Visionary Wish List has been created, regularly reviewed with Integrator, and is being fulfilled.	☐	
	3-Piece Puzzle mapped. Knows how their "edges" fit with both their business and their Integrator.	☐	

Pillars	Mindsets		1-10
2. Warrior Shape	Understands that taking care of themselves is not a selfish act.	☐	
	Prioritizes consistent care of their body through sleep, nutrition, movement, and recovery.	☐	
	Protects mental clarity and confidence by taking regular Clarity Breaks.	☐	
	Grounds their spirit by remaining intentionally connected to their greater "why."	☐	
3. Surround Yourself	Has filled each of the Seven Posts effectively and is confident that all are performing well.	☐	
	Quickly addresses any gaps that may develop in the Seven Posts.	☐	
	Has identified the Seven Forces— the vital human relationships in their world—and can name at least one person for each.	☐	
	Invests intentionally in each Seven Forces relationship, building trust, rhythm, and clarity.	☐	
	Has built a solid "shield wall" to effectively protect them from unexpected chaos and external threats.	☐	

Pillars	Mindsets		1-10
4. Commit to Your Operating System	Committed to an Individual OS (e.g., 9 Domains of Freedom[IP*]) to manage their energy, time, and focus.	☐	
	Uses the Visionary OS (10 Pillars) to guide decisions and behavior in their Visionary role.	☐	
	Employs a V/I Duo OS (5 Rules). Partnered with an Integrator and striving to maximize the power of their V/I Duo.	☐	
	Leads within a defined Business OS (e.g., EOS), and is a role model of commitment to that system.	☐	
5. Support Your Integrator	Climbing the OS Ladder[IP].	☐	
	Consistently shows public support for their Integrator.	☐	
	Wants the Integrator to win and is doing their part to make that outcome real.	☐	
	Fully committed to the Same Page Meeting and uses it to strengthen clarity, resolve tension, and reinforce alignment.	☐	
	Challenges the Integrator in healthy ways, but avoids patterns of sabotage, tampering, or withholding.	☐	
	Using the V/I Tools (RFPI, IRC, VRC). Completed and discussed every ninety days (at least), with steadily improving alignment and scores.	☐	

Pillars	Mindsets		1-10
6. Think About What You Think About	Intentionally shifts their thoughts away from things that are harmful, toward things that are helpful.	☐	
	Demonstrates patience, especially in moments of uncertainty, challenge, or transition.	☐	
	Avoids Out to Pasture thinking. Instead chooses to stay engaged and relevant.	☐	
	Cultivates an attitude of gratitude.	☐	
	Embraces intellectual humility, remaining open to learn and discover different perspectives.	☐	
	Chooses to develop a foundation of trust (vs. control), especially with the Integrator.	☐	
	Provides guidance without tampering, giving direction while honoring others' accountability.	☐	
	Blends their divergent thinking with the Integrator's convergent thinking, effectively converting valuable ideas into execution.	☐	
7. Watch Out for Pitfalls	Avoids bad behavior (tampering, end runs, playing the owner card, etc.).	☐	
	No longer feels put Out to Pasture. Embraces their Intrinsic Genius*.	☐	
	Avoids Imposter Syndrome. Recognizes they've earned the right to be where they are	☐	

Pillars	Mindsets		1-10
	Avoids becoming the bottleneck. Knows when and where to let go.	☐	
	Avoids isolation. Knows they are not alone.	☐	
	Seeks support early. Uses personal warning signs to recognize and stop harmful behaviors before they cause damage.	☐	
8. Help Others Stretch	Stretches others to the Ledge of Conceivability*, not by pushing harder, but by expanding belief.	☐	
	Balances aspiration with clarity; stretches just far enough to inspire, without overreaching.	☐	
	Ensures that the long-term vision is grounded in reality, but not constrained by it.	☐	
	Ensures everyone understands and supports the 10-Year Target.	☐	
	Embraces the discipline of prediction; sets clear targets with 80 percent confidence on the Traction side of the plan.	☐	
	Inspires others with big ideas, then partners with the Integrator to bring them down to earth.	☐	
9. Go Slow to Go Fast	Spots and tames their default frenetic patterns before they kill momentum.	☐	
	Resets quickly when their own behavior creates unnecessary chaos.	☐	
	Leverages focus to trigger flow within the team.	☐	

Pillars	Mindsets		1-10
	Understands the Traffic Jam Theory[IP]; works hard to prevent bottlenecks and protect flow.	☐	
	Slows down on purpose in meetings and at home to get better results.	☐	
10. Do No Harm	Recognizes that avoiding harm is a leadership discipline and a prerequisite for sustainable freedom.	☐	
	Holds themselves accountable for consistency and clarity in vision. Makes this a priority.	☐	
	Does not waffle or send mixed signals.	☐	
	Does not undermine the structure with special exemptions.	☐	
	Signals an "alert" when thinking out loud, so teams don't mistake it for new marching orders.	☐	
	Uses the Decision Tree** to empower leaders to make decisions with accountability.	☐	
Total Score:			

*This segment is drawn from the Exponential Freedom[IP] model 2014-2025 Copyright Peloton Creations LLC. Exponential Freedom is a trademark of Peloton Creations LLC. All rights reserved. Used with permission.

**Decision Tree credited to Fierce Conversations by Susan Scott.

Remember, we're using this as a tool to check how we're doing.

Pillar 1: Know Thyself

- ☐ Profile results identified (Kolbe, Culture Index, Working Genius, etc.) and using them to guide decision-making and alignment.
- ☐ Intrinsic Genius (personal combination of competence, joy, and drive) defined.
- ☐ Joy/Competence Matrix done regularly, enabling Visionary to stay in their "sweet spot."
- ☐ Visionary Wish List has been created, regularly reviewed with Integrator, and is being fulfilled.
- ☐ 3-Piece Puzzle mapped. Knows how their "edges" fit with both their business and their Integrator.

You'll see some of the mindsets that we just discussed. Read through these mindsets and consider whether you feel you've got a good handle on each area. If you're doing terribly at one, don't check that box. If you're doing okay, put a slash, like a spare in bowling. If you're doing really well, give yourself a full "X."

Let's go through this one together.

- ☐ "Profile results identified (Kolbe, Culture Index, Working Genius, etc.) and using them to guide decision-making and alignment."

  If you're doing well on that, give yourself an "X." If not, give yourself a spare, or an empty frame.

- ☐ "Intrinsic Genius (personal combination of competence, joy, and drive) defined."

Have you completed your Intrinsic Genius? Do you love it? Are you increasingly spending more time there?

☐ "Joy/Competence Matrix done regularly, enabling Visionary to stay in their 'sweet spot.'"

Are you using this tool quarterly? Delegating at least one activity that falls outside your sweet spot?

☐ "The Visionary Wish List has been created, and they're working with the Integrator to fulfill it."

Have you created that wish list? Have you started the conversation with your Integrator? Are you compartmentalizing the items and taking steps to make them happen?

☐ "3-Piece Puzzle mapped. Knows how their 'edges' fit with both their business and their Integrator."

Are you the right Visionary for this business? Have you backed into the shape of your Integrator piece? Have you found them? Do you "click" with them?

Mark each box appropriately for wherever you're at—no judgment here—X, slash, or empty. The key is to be completely honest with yourself. Mark it down. This is your starting point. And then, give yourself a score of how well you feel you're doing overall, based on considering the mindsets for this Pillar. The scale is 1–10, with 10 being the highest. If you're nailing it, you're a 10; the lowest you can be is a 1. Most of you are likely somewhere in between.

You've done the work. You've looked in the mirror, surfaced your patterns, clarified your Intrinsic Genius, and begun solving for your ideal Duo Fit. This is your foundation. Every other Pillar will build from this one— so come back to it often. The better you know yourself, the stronger every part of your Visionary journey will become. You are the constant in every part of your business. When you're anchored in who you are, everything else can move forward with clarity.

Now that you know more about yourself as a Visionary, let's move on to Pillar 2: Maintain Warrior Shape. The Visionary's road is hard. You'll need to be in warrior shape. Let's explore taking care of yourself in a way that enables you to show up and fully bring your intrinsic genius.

PILLAR 2

MAINTAIN WARRIOR SHAPE

You can't pour from an empty cup.

—Unknown

As a Visionary entrepreneur, you have a wide circle of people who depend on you—employees, customers, partners, investors, communities, and even your own family. They're all counting on you to be at your best. If you're not, they will suffer.

I feel compelled to highlight this pillar early on because of a certain behavior pattern I've noticed many times. And science backs it up. According to a 2015 article in *Harvard Business Review*, a range of academic studies showed that leaders with higher well-being scores—including physical and emotional health—performed better across leadership capacity, decision-making, and business outcomes.[1]

There's something instinctive about many Visionary entrepreneurs—they default to a setting of self-sacrifice. They show up earlier, stay later, work harder, and miss family events. They forego a paycheck to make sure others get paid. Maybe they put in even more money by pulling from their personal credit card.

Some sacrifice could certainly be considered good. Perhaps even admirable. Yet it can't go on forever at that level. It's not healthy nor sustainable. It's not what you signed up for when you started this thing.

It's likely no surprise that Visionaries also report higher rates of anxiety, depression, addiction, and other forms of unhealthy excess. A 2015 study published in the *Journal of Business Venturing* found nearly half of entrepreneurs surveyed had experienced a mental health condition.[2] This wiring fuels greatness, but it comes with risk. If you don't manage it, it will manage you.

Michael was the Visionary for a high-tech software company. He was one of six owners, with about eighteen employees. While their technology was excellent, they were growing at a pace that kept causing cash-flow crunches. As soon as they'd dig out of one, they'd find

---

[1] Seppälä, E. and K. Cameron. "Proof That Positive Work Cultures Are More Productive." *Harvard Business Review.* December 1, 2015. https://hbr.org/2015/12/proof-that-positive-work-cultures-are-more-productive.

[2] Freeman, M. A., S. L. Johnson, P. J. Staudenmaier, and K. Ronning. "Are Entrepreneurs 'Touched with Fire'?" *Journal of Business Venturing* 30, no. 1 (2015): 1–11. https://doi.org/10.1016/j.jbusvent.2014.06.003.

themselves right back in another. The pace was grueling. Michael knew he was asking a lot of everyone, and he felt some level of guilt about this. His response was to double down with his own time and money. He committed to himself that nobody would work more than he did. And nobody would suffer more financially. As you might imagine, some of this was good. It set a certain tone for the rest of the team. "Whatever it takes! I'm willing, are you?"

However, as time went on, the sacrifices compounded. The negative side of these choices began to emerge. More time spent at work was not better time. It wasn't really more productive or valuable. In fact, Michael's productivity actually decreased. His energy fell. His health began to suffer. He stressed over family dynamics resulting from his excessive time away. And his financial sacrifices made the family matters even worse. His wife was distraught to learn that he'd pulled another credit line to cover another payroll. And when they went together to pull out a second mortgage, to cover yet another shortfall, that almost broke their marriage.

Michael's body began to fail him. His mind fragmented and scattered, and his spirit was broken. It was almost impossible to see the way out. This reality could not be further from what he envisioned when he took this entrepreneurial leap.

If the company goes down, everyone goes down. Every stakeholder pays a price. Some more than others, no doubt, but all get hurt. Employees are back on the street. Investors lose their money. Customers can't find the support they need for a product on which they've grown to depend. The list goes on. And Michael is likely hurt most of all. Financial ruin? Divorce? Psychological scarring? What will his children think of him after such a failure?

Fortunately, an acquisition bailed them out—and just in time. Michael and the team held on long enough to get the deal done, secure a much-needed payday, and escape the suffocating cash-flow cycle that had nearly drowned them. It just as easily could've ended in disaster.

Know that there's a better way. It involves preparation. Adversity will come in whatever form (cash flow, people, product, competition, etc.). You can count on it. To be your best in the Visionary role, you must be in "warrior shape" when it does. To do this, you'll need to overcome your instinctive pattern of self-sacrifice and push into the mode of self-care for the greater good.

To help you get there, I'll draw from a framework I developed over a decade ago: the Exponential Freedom[IP] model and the 9 Domains of Freedom[IP]. Think of the framework as a Personal Operating System (OS) for humans. While this is a business book, Visionary entrepreneurs are also human. And how you take care of yourself as a person directly impacts your ability to perform in the specific role of Visionary. It is all interrelated. While the full depth of the Exponential Freedom model is beyond the scope of this book, I have created a high-level version—as a special bonus mini-book for you—available online.

VisionaryBook.com

As we think about maintaining Warrior Shape, you may recall the pre-flight airline announcement about oxygen masks. "Always mask yourself first—before you help your kids or others." That message illustrates an important idea for Visionaries to consider: If you don't take care of yourself, how can you expect to take care of anybody else? This is not selfish! You take this approach to ensure the greater good of all stakeholders.

Being in Warrior Shape requires you to proactively "care" for certain foundational areas so you can effectively take care of anybody—or anything—else. So what are these areas? Well, at birth, we all start out with the same three gifts:

- your body
- your mind
- your spirit (or soul or energy, however you label it)

These three areas will never matter more to *anyone* else than they do to *you*. If you don't "care" for them, you can't expect others to "care" for you. It is vital for you to "Own Your Experience" in this respect. Literally, everything else depends on it!

It's easy to neglect yourself in these areas because you have so many other worthy (and urgent) demands for your limited time: the new product launch, expanding the sales team, or that new market you're entering. This list goes on and on. In the beginning, you may feel that you're doing okay in each of those three personal areas. Of course, you can always come back around and work on them later. Right? Well, yes, you can—until you can't.

How do you decide where to spend your time and energy? You've probably seen this Eisenhower matrix at some point. It helps you think about where things fall in relation to both their importance and their urgency.

EISENHOWER MATRIX

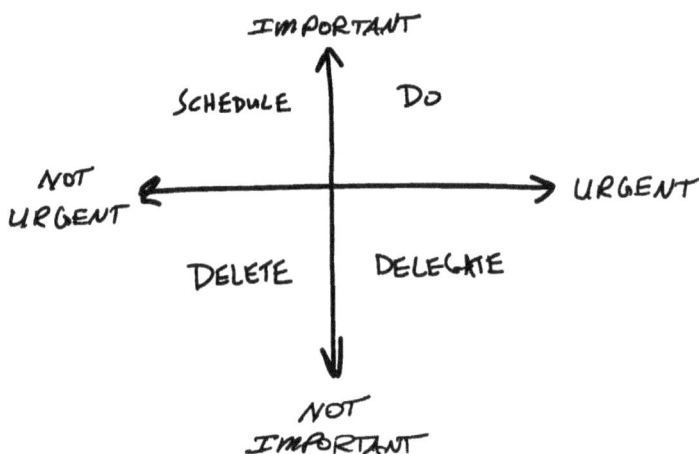

IMPORTANT

SCHEDULE   DO

NOT URGENT ← → URGENT

DELETE   DELEGATE

NOT IMPORTANT

—mcw

Most Visionaries live in firefighting mode—always solving what's both Urgent and Important. But that means they rarely get to what's Important but not

Urgent. Until it bites them. Something breaks. And by then, the cost of repair is 10X what it would've taken to prevent it. If you knew the true price in advance, you never would've made that trade. You'd never have accepted a free pass on nutrition if you knew it led to adult-onset diabetes. Much less all those sleepless nights that eventually led to a stroke.

For each of these three foundational areas, your Present Self must have a candid discussion with your Future Self. Project yourself into the future—far enough where you'll be notably different from your Present Self. Pick an age where you'll be wiser, having the benefit and perspective of your added experience. If you're thirty now, maybe fifty-five is a good reference. If you're sixty, maybe go out to seventy-five. You pick the specific age of your Future Self.

Now take that short-term question you have, and imagine querying your older, wiser Future Self about it. Which option would they want you to pick? Why? Keep in mind that Future Self has a vested interest in the outcome in all respects. The only difference between the two of you is time. Less money now, for better relationships later? Lots of fun now, for less money later? Eating like a pig now, for endless health battles later? These are very healthy discussions to have with your Future Self. Remember, they are you. Heed their wisdom.

From this thought exercise, formulate a picture of the future you actually want. What needs to be true for your Future Self, for you to feel excited about that future? Do this for each of the three foundational areas. Then, from that anchor point on the future horizon, we can draw a line back to today. We capture a baseline for our Present Self, then mark milestones at various points along the way to the Future Self we really want.

For Body as an example, when my Future Self is seventy, I weigh 180 pounds at 20 percent body fat, or better. I can do fifty pushups nonstop and still run/walk five miles per day without excessive effort. And I can throw a football twenty yards, or better, playing catch with my kids and grandkids.

Meanwhile, my Present Self is fifty. I weigh 195 at 22 percent body fat. I can do fifty nonstop pushups and run/walk five miles per day with ease. My shoulders are in pretty bad shape. I can't really throw a football without extreme pain.

So if I'm going to get to my target by seventy, I've got some work to do. My strength training and nutrition programs both need to improve. In addition to a revised plan, my trainer will help me set specific goals for future dates to help me stay on track. I'll also need to keep up with my running, which is currently a habit. What other habits will support each of my goals in this area? In addition, I'll either need physical therapy or possibly even surgery for my shoulders. Neither will be easy. But they're important to me. And if I start now, I can reach those goals, which is attractive and motivating for me. On the other hand, if I wait ten more years to start, that Future Self may get completely out of reach. I do not want to experience that type of regret.

In each area, consider the possibilities. What are some examples of future outcomes I might enjoy? What "levers" are available to me that will increase the odds of achieving my desired outcomes? What things can I measure so I can easily track my progress along the way? And finally, what activities along this path can I convert to habits, nudging me closer to that attractive future day after day?

Your Body

A Visionary body in Warrior Shape is fit. You don't get sick, which means you don't miss. As I've seen posted in a few college locker rooms, "The most important ability is availability." You show up—as promised—every time. You have endurance. You show up with strong energy and intensity. You have mobility; if we need to move for travel or otherwise, you are not the hold-up. Aesthetically, you look your best. As the external face of the company, outsiders see you as a healthy embodiment of the physical image you want to project. What do you see today when you look in the mirror? Bottom line, you must be able to engage steadily and deliver the vital contributions your role requires. The business simply can't get these from anywhere else.

That's a near-term view of how we might describe your Future Self in this area. Can you say that all these things are true for you today? If yes, are you doing what's required to keep it so? If not, then it's time to get to work.

What levers do we have available to help us move from our Present Self toward this Future Self we've chosen to pursue? Fortunately, there's much written about this particular area. To avoid being overwhelmed by all the possibilities these experts proclaim, let me boil it all down to the simplest version I can imagine: Fitness. Nutrition. Sleep. All of the literature seems to fall under one of these three categories.

You must create a simple plan for each that you will follow. Don't overreach. Just pick something. And get started. Remember the old saying, "The best time to plant a tree is twenty years ago; the next best time is today."

For example, your simple plan might be something like this:

1. Do something physical every day.

   Strength training, movement, stretching, yoga, etc.

2. Eat smart on weekdays.

   Avoid sugar. Limit alcohol.

3. Get 7–8 hours of sleep most nights.

   Pre-bedtime ritual. Optimize sleeping area. Consistent wake time.

For each of these, you can also set specific objectives over time. You can identify measurables that will help you keep track. And you can identify daily and weekly habits that will help you stick to your plan. There are also countless tools available. Most people already have a watch with more fitness tracking/coaching capabilities than they'll ever use.

Importantly, don't let the need for the perfect plan hold you back. Don't get distracted by looking for the perfect tool. Just start. Do something. Keep it simple. Any improvement here is better than nothing.

Remember, you only get one body. And what an amazing creation it is. The human body may well be the most amazing creation ever, so we'd better take care of it!

Your Mind

A Visionary mind in Warrior Shape is clear and confident. You are mentally and emotionally ready for any challenge and whatever adversity may come along with it. You are resilient. You live in a combined state of grit, focus, courage, and determination.

Your mind is a powerful cognitive engine. Your processor works at lightning speed. It is sharp and clear and never feels "gummed up." Your mind is easily focused, rather than fragmented and scattered. And you are clearly focused on goals in areas that interest and excite you. Those offer the best puzzles to solve.

Your working memory is fast and reliable. You have the ability to recall facts, figures, names, and other useful pieces of information. Seemingly, this information comes to you effortlessly, in the moment, whenever you need it.

Your mental storage capacity seems almost unlimited. Knowledge and wisdom have built up over years of experience. And you're adding a little more to the library every day. Meanwhile, this amazing brain of yours is always cross-referencing, connecting, and re-organizing everything to provide you with increasingly powerful insights.

In addition, you're a lifelong learner. Curious and consistent. You seek out new ideas and approaches, explore them, and look for ways to apply them. You know how you learn best, and you make it a habit to do so with regularity. Always building that learning muscle as you go.

So what levers do we have to help us create and sustain such a mind? Again, let's keep it simple. You have many options to choose from. A simple plan here may include clarity, cognition, and learning.

Again, form a simple plan, and get started. For example:

1. **Clarity.** I always know what's important and where I should focus my attention.

   Planning routines, checklists, schedules.

2. **Cognition.** I do something daily to exercise my "brain muscle."

   Mental games, intellectual challenges, creative sessions.

3. **Learning.** I read one new book every month and teach someone else about it.

   Book summaries, audiobooks, online courses.

Identify and employ the most useful measurables and tools to help you. Avoid the dual trap of perfection and complexity and start! Drive toward daily and weekly habits that "pre-decide" these activities for you. Having already decided that this is what you do, you just do it. This is more sustainable than facing the same decision every day, such as "Am I going to do this today?" Avoid the mental fatigue, and decide in advance.

One example of such a "habit" is Jeff Bezos's 1-Hour Rule. This is a daily morning practice where he dedicates his first hour after waking to screen-free, relaxed activities. He calls this "puttering." He might sip coffee, read the paper, or have breakfast with his family. Importantly, this time specifically excludes checking phones or digital devices. This routine creates a slow and gentle start for him, protecting mental energy for enhanced decision-making throughout the day. Neuroscience supports this approach, showing benefits to brain health, memory, and mental clarity, all while reducing cognitive overload.

As for tools, one relevant example for keeping your mind in Warrior Shape is an EOS tool called the Clarity Break. The onslaught of issues coming at you left and right does not stop. Imagine a giant spigot hanging over your head, and someone has cranked it open. The flow keeps coming, and coming, and coming, and the downward pressure can become overwhelming.

Have you felt that before? When you're in that moment, being pressed down under the oncoming flow of demands, in which direction is your confidence going?

I've asked thousands of leaders this question, and the majority respond instantly with a "thumbs down" signal.

To make matters even worse, who's depending on you to help them with their confidence? You guessed it—everybody else in the organization. If your confidence is wavering, you won't be effective at helping others charge ahead with their own confidence.

To be proactive in protecting and building our confidence, we need to be diligent about taking Clarity Breaks, a systematic approach to managing our clarity.

If we scroll through history, every great leader has used some form of this approach. Bill Gates famously has his "Think Week." Ben Franklin and Mahatma Gandhi were also known for systematic reflection.

Your Clarity Break doesn't need to be exactly like someone else's—it just needs to work for you. You must pick a time and a place, and make it happen. For example, I like to do mine on Friday mornings. I go to a specific Starbucks and bring my notepad, a pen, and noise-canceling earbuds. I also have an app on my phone called Focus@Will, which is designed to get my brain in an alpha thinking state. It plays digital music—without the distraction of lyrics—which is what works well for me.

I block out ninety minutes—where nobody can interrupt me, bother me, or make any requests of me. I keep that time sacred, dedicated to only my Clarity Break.

I don't have any specific plan ahead of time. I just write down whatever comes to me. Then, as other thoughts, ideas, or other things come, I write those down too.

On some days—at the end of the ninety minutes—I'll have written seven bullet points. On others, I'll have written seven pages. Your subconscious knows what it needs to get out. It just needs the space to do so. The Clarity Break is about intentionally giving your whole brain that space to unpack.

How do you think Clarity Breaks impact your confidence? It drives it up. Your clarity and focus climb higher. You remind yourself of what's important. You know what to do—and that is something you can *feel!*

As I teach this tool, I recommend that people not take Clarity Breaks at their house or work, or any other place where they'll be prone to distractions. However, you may vary your method. I had one client who used a whiteboard instead of a notepad. The whiteboard was essentially his brain. It hung on the wall facing his desk. He liked to take his Clarity Breaks every two weeks. He'd start by completely clearing the whiteboard of his previous brain dump. (That feels kinda scary to some people.) Then he'd sit back and examine the whiteboard. Walk over, add to it, and sit back down again. Get back up, capture another thought, then go back to his seat.

Repeating this for ninety minutes, which was how long he protected for his Clarity Breaks. During those sessions, he'd completely rebuild his brain, enabling him to refocus and gain the clarity he needed to be a great Visionary.

That's essentially what you're doing in a Clarity Break—stepping back to think will create clarity for you and restore your confidence. All great leaders practice this discipline on a regular basis, and it's one I hope you will routinely put into practice.

Clarity Break™ Questions

- Is the Vision and Plan for the business/department on track?
- What is the number one goal?
- Am I focusing on the most important things?
- Do I have the Right People in the Right Seats to grow?
- What is the one "people move" that I must make this quarter?
- How strong is my bench?
- If I lose a key player, do I have someone ready to fill the seat?
- Are my processes working well?
- What seems overly complicated that must be simplified?
- Do I understand what my direct reports truly love to do and are great at doing?
- Am I leveraging their strengths?
- What can I delegate to others in order to use my time more effectively?
- What can we do to be more proactive versus being reactive?
- What can I do to improve communication?
- What's my top priority this week? This month?

Your Spirit

A Visionary spirit in Warrior Shape is energized, centered, and connected. You are completely aligned with your purpose. Your actions match your words. Your words match your thoughts. Your thoughts match your feelings. Everything is integrated. This strength of spirit gives you great courage, rooted in confidence and belief. Your willingness to sacrifice for the greater good rests on this same foundation. You feel connected to something larger than yourself. You know it's all about more than just you.

Some people refer to this domain as their soul or their energy. Whatever you call it, it's essential to tend to it. What levers influence your Spirit? In simple terms, think of what you might already do to tend to your soul. Perhaps you meditate, belong to a church, or keep a journal.

Building on that, here are five powerful levers you can focus on to build a simple plan that strengthens your Spirit—bringing it into warrior shape:

1. **Purpose Alignment.** *Clarify it. Own it. Live it.*

   When your daily actions reconnect you to your deeper Why, your spirit gains clarity and momentum. This requires regularly revisiting your Intrinsic Genius, refining your vision, and making sure that key decisions and priorities align with both. Drift happens. That's natural. This lever pulls you back to center.

2. **Integrity Practices.** *Make your word law—and treat it as sacred.*

   Integrity occurs when thought, feeling, word, and action all line up. Strengthening this lever means: Keeping promises, especially to yourself. Saying no when something violates your values. Speaking truth, even when it's uncomfortable. This builds spiritual power and trust in yourself and from others.

3. **Renewal Rituals.** *Energy doesn't come from hustle—it comes from rhythm.*

   Your spirit needs rhythm: time to rest, reflect, and reconnect. Rituals like solitude, nature immersion, prayer, meditation, journaling, or breathwork help you stay emotionally grounded and spiritually charged. This is how a warrior heals and recenters between battles.

4. **Sacred Sacrifice.** *Choose what matters most—and be willing to pay the price.*

   Warrior spirit is strengthened by voluntary sacrifice for a meaningful cause. Whether it's time, comfort, money, or ego. What you willingly give up for your vision becomes fuel for the soul. This lever is about intentionality, not your instincts: don't just grind—consecrate your effort. If you're going to sacrifice, make it meaningful.

5. **Higher Connection.** *It's not just about you. That's the point.*

   This lever pulls you into a relationship with something greater—God, the Universe, legacy, your tribe. Whatever language you use, a spiritual connection lifts your perspective above self-interest and strengthens your resilience. You begin to lead not just with ambition, but with reverence.

You might be surprised to learn that there are measurables and tools to help you in the Spirit domain. Measurables are easy when you look for the primary daily/weekly activity underneath whatever you're trying to accomplish: journal entries, prayer/meditation sessions, church attendance, and so on. Just look for the activity or behavior you commit to practice.

And remember, we're driving everything toward habits. As an example, my Daily Habits checklist includes: morning journal/reflection, scripture study, and prayer/meditation. I literally have these on an app called "Habit List," along with seventeen other things, many of which are related to the foundational Body, Mind, and Spirit domains. Every day, I do my best to check each of them off at some point during the day. And I'm not perfect—far from it. However, I do have a focus on these specific habits. And a system to bring them to the top of mind every day. With that, my odds of actually taking action are 100X higher than if I simply read the idea in a book, thought it was good, then let it float on down the river. If it makes sense to you, simplify it and put it into action.

If you're looking for a practical framework to strengthen your Spirit domain and bring it into warrior shape, I highly recommend The 10 Disciplines program by Gino Wickman. It offers a set of powerful, actionable habits designed to help driven entrepreneurs stay centered, present, and connected to their higher purpose. Gino's tools complement the levers outlined here and provide a strong daily structure for building long-term spiritual strength, clarity, and inner peace. For a deeper dive, explore his book or training program at the10disciplines.com.

Transformation

For this exercise, you'll see the three foundational areas of Warrior Shape listed below:

AREA	IMPORTANCE (1–10)	HABITS (Current / New)	PERFORMANCE (1–10)
BODY			
MIND			
SPIRIT			

First, score each area in order of importance to you as you see it today. The scale is 1–10, with 10 indicating that it's the most important.

Next, write down any current habits you have that support you in this area. And then note any new habits you'd like to establish.

Finally, rate yourself on how you're doing right now. This is your current reality—how you're performing in each of these three foundational areas today. Again, the scale ranges from 1–10, with 10 being the best.

Sit back and evaluate what you see:
- Where do you see yourself performing the best?
- Where is your biggest gap—the area where you have the greatest opportunity to improve?
- How do you feel about the area you rated lowest in importance?
- How does your Future Self feel about it?
- Which new habits will you actually implement?
- Which old habits will you re-invigorate?

Based on this new perspective, what's one move you will commit to making in the next ninety days? Write it down. And do it.

Frank completed this exercise and was struck by how poorly he was doing in the Spirit area. He was dedicated to Body and Mind, giving himself a 10 on both in terms of Importance and a 9 on both in terms of Performance. He also wanted to rank Spirit highly in Importance, but he just wasn't doing anything in that area. And he wasn't sure he was ready to commit to any changes.

He thought about his seventy-five-year-old Future Self and imagined him looking back on his fifty-year-old Present Self. Frank could well imagine what he'd consider most important at that future stage of his life, and that would be his eternal soul. His Present Self could feel this tug-of-war at hand between the Present and the Future. It actually became rather uncomfortable for him. In the end, he decided to rank Spirit with an Importance of 8, not the 10 his Future Self wanted, but important enough for him to get started in that area of his life. He committed to add a daily practice of reading a brief scripture devotional, followed by a prayer. This is something he had done when he was younger, but had drifted away from over the years. Drift happens. Perhaps this small change would "prime the pump" for doing even more in this area.

Now let's take an inventory of how you're doing on this Pillar.

Pillar 2: Warrior Shape

☐ Understands that taking care of themselves is not a selfish act.

☐ Prioritizes consistent care of their body through sleep, nutrition, movement, and recovery.

☐ Protects mental clarity and confidence by taking regular Clarity Breaks.

☐ Grounds their spirit by remaining intentionally connected to their greater "why."

Now review your Visionary Report Card and read through the mindsets listed above for Pillar 2. As you did before, put an X on the things you're doing great with, a slash for things you're doing so-so with, and leave blank the areas that you still have to work on. Then, rate yourself on how you're doing for Pillar 2. The scale is 1–10, with 10 being the highest.

Onward to Pillar 3: Surround Yourself.

PILLAR 3

SURROUND YOURSELF

*It is not the strength of the individual players,
but the strength of the unit—and how
they all function together.*

—Bill Belichick

Have you seen the movie *300*? It features the famous
Battle of Thermopylae in ancient Greece between the
Spartans and the invading Persians. The battle takes
place in a narrow mountain pass chosen because it
offered the strategic advantage to help the Greeks defend
against a much larger invading force. The Spartans,
known for their military prowess, employed a military
tactic called the phalanx formation. The phalanx was
formed by hoplites (citizen-soldiers who fought with
shields and spears) arranged in rows typically eight
deep, creating a thick wall of shields. Such a tight formation was challenging for opposing forces to break

through. In one of the famous scenes from the movie, King Leonidas of Sparta calls out to his men with the command: "Shield wall!" That's exactly what you need.

The role of a Visionary entrepreneur is fraught with peril. You spend time, mentally and physically, out on the frontier, which can be a dangerous place. Some people don't want you to venture too far out. The change you create there makes them feel uncomfortable. Others are threatened by your presence. They may see you as an invader on their turf. Many simply don't understand what you're trying to do. In each case, their drive for self-preservation creates a force of opposition.

These forces can mount up against you, sometimes in league with each other, to stop you. To distract you. To hurt you. To slow you down. To make you doubt yourself.

Some opposition forces you can see clearly, while others are stealthy and attack from within—via your own thoughts. They come from all directions. You've fought them off in the past. You're likely dealing with some at the present. And yet more lies ahead in your future. You must protect yourself.

Pillar 3 is a call to surround yourself with people who can protect you from these negative forces. You can think of these people as your "shield wall." You need your own version of a phalanx formation.

You won't survive long on the frontier without real protection. This isn't just about roles; it's about resilience. Each of these posts plays a different role, but together they form the barrier between you and the chaos trying to take you down. A solid shield wall is the difference between pushing forward or being forced to retreat. There are seven vital posts around your wall. Some are filled by one person. Some require a team. Regardless, make sure each is filled with strength.

The Seven Posts

First, let's meet the seven vital posts that will make up your shield wall. Each of these different types of posts represents an opportunity to counteract those negative forces, or "headwinds," that you will encounter as a Visionary. These posts all exist right now; you just may not have them all filled at this moment, or maybe not with the right person. Any vacant post is a vulnerability, as is relying on someone too weak to fill it for you.

The people in these posts are your allies. They appear consistently with you, not just stepping in and out of your life. Some of them were very hard to find, while some of them sought you out. Others have been mysteriously brought into your life, perhaps just when you needed them most. You want these allies to surround you and protect you at all times. Can you guess which posts you need on this wall?

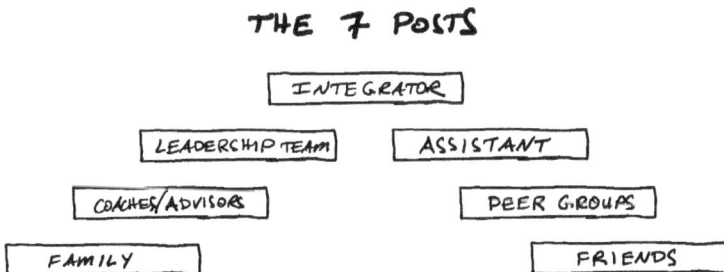

THE 7 POSTS

INTEGRATOR

LEADERSHIP TEAM   ASSISTANT

COACHES/ADVISORS   PEER GROUPS

FAMILY   FRIENDS

– Mcw

Allow me to introduce each one in turn.

Integrator

First, and this should come as no surprise: your
Integrator. A great one can change your life. We've
already talked at length about all the different ways
your Integrator protects you and helps you leverage your
Intrinsic Genius. Make sure that you have someone very
strong manning that post, and that you are working
diligently to maximize the power of your relationship
with them.

Jake had been sitting in the Visionary and Integrator
seats for years. His name was literally on the company,
and he'd convinced himself this meant everyone had to
speak personally with him. Eventually, he was able to
get the right Integrator in that seat. It changed everything. When I asked him to describe the feeling, he
exclaimed, "I no longer have to be the fireman!" Every
upset customer, vendor, or employee stopped hitting
his desk first. He still got involved when truly appropriate, which was less than 20 percent of the amount
he'd been doing.

Leadership Team

Your business must have a leadership team, the group
of leaders who sit atop the organization. Along with
the Visionary and the Integrator, they are charged with
the long-term good of the entire business. Each of
them is charged with a specific set of core roles. In the
simplest form, you have a leader for Marketing and
Sales. Another for Operations. And one for Finance/

Administration. Maybe you divide your structure a bit more. In any case, think of these as the leadership team "seats."

In its classic form, Marketing should make the world aware of your business and the promise of value you can provide. Marketing generates leads to pursue. Sales needs to convert those leads into customers (or clients). Once converted, they become the responsibility of Operations, which "keeps the promise" by delivering the value that you sold and perhaps making your product. Meanwhile, Finance/Administration concentrates on keeping track and providing the infrastructure support the other functions need. This helps each of them stay clearly focused on the "main thing" we need them to do (e.g., lead gen, sales, delivery).

A business can't afford to be weak in any of these areas. Each one makes a vital contribution toward your ability to succeed.

Now close your eyes for a moment and picture all the "seats" of your leadership team, along with the person currently sitting in it. Focus on the leader who's accountable for each of those areas. Study their face. Look deep into their eyes. You may see the same person sitting in more than one of those seats. Maybe you see yourself staring back at you from one (or more) of them.

With that picture anchored clearly in your mind, can you say without a doubt that you have rock stars for every single seat on your leadership team?

Be brutally honest, really think about it.

Often, given this level of scrutiny, you will realize that someone currently on your leadership team isn't the rock star that you need. And that's holding you back. It slows you down. It keeps you from getting to the next level you want to achieve.

The Culture Formula[IP]

Before we dive into diagnosing the pace of your leadership team, it's important to zoom out and look at the broader system they're operating within. Specifically, your culture.

I've worked with thousands of entrepreneurial companies, and I can't tell you how often I hear leaders enthusiastically describe their "amazing culture," only to discover toxic turnover, missed targets, and team dysfunction just below the surface. Too often, culture is confused with perks. Ping-pong tables. Craft beer on tap. Inspirational posters on the wall. But those are all just signals, not real substance.

THE CULTURE FORMULA

$$\left[\begin{matrix} \text{CRYSTAL CLEAR} \\ \text{EXPECTATIONS} \\ \hline \text{CORE VALUES} \\ + \\ \text{CORE SEAT ROLES} \end{matrix}\right] \times \left[\begin{matrix} \text{CONSISTENT} \\ \text{ACCOUNTABILITY} \\ \hline \text{LEADERSHIP} \\ + \\ \text{MANAGEMENT} \end{matrix}\right] = \begin{matrix} \text{ACTUAL} \\ \text{CULTURE} \end{matrix}$$

—MCW

The real foundation of culture is built through clarity and consistent accountability. There's a formula I've developed over time that captures exactly how strong culture is created:

The Culture Formula

Crystal Clear Expectations

(Core Values + Core Seat Roles)

x

Consistent Accountability

(Leadership + Management)

= Actual Culture

This is more than just a clever equation. It's how healthy cultures are systemically built and reinforced. The first half of the formula—crystal clear expectations—means every person in your organization knows exactly how they're expected to show up (Core Values) and exactly what they're responsible for delivering (Core Roles). The second half—consistent accountability—means those expectations are upheld through strong leadership and management. EOS refers to this as LMA (leading, managing, and holding people accountable).

When this system is functioning properly, culture becomes self-regulating. Those who fit both your values and their seat will thrive. While those who don't will tend to self-eject. Exceptions can't survive—not because of micromanagement but because the culture itself rejects it, like an immune system targeting a virus.

When you surround yourself with the right people, in the right seats, held to the right expectations, you unlock the full power of your team. And that's exactly what we're going to measure next, with the Leadership Speedometer[IP].

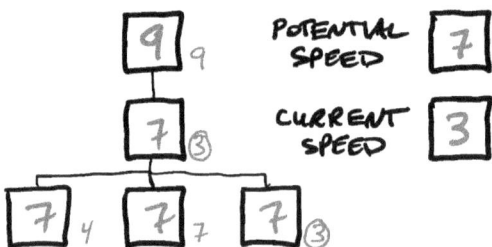

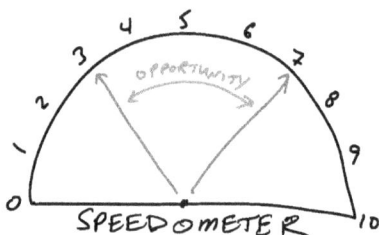

The Leadership Speedometer

This is a diagnostic tool for identifying the bottlenecks in your leadership team.

Imagine your leadership team as a stagecoach pulled by five horses. Each horse represents one of your key leaders. Now ask yourself: "How fast can our stagecoach really go?"

The answer is simple: only as fast as the slowest horse. That's what the Leadership Speedometer measures. Too often, Visionaries get frustrated by their team's inability to go fast. But they haven't identified the actual drag. Sometimes the issue is a weak link. Sometimes it's a strong leader who's spread too thin. Sometimes it's both.

Here's how the tool works...

Each leader identifies:

- The specific seats they're currently responsible for—Integrator, Ops, Finance, Sales, and so on. This includes *all* seats they occupy across the Accountability Chart, not just leadership team seats.
- A "fit rating" for each seat. How well they truly fit the core roles of each seat. Are they intrinsically wired for it? Is that the seat they want most? Do they have the experience, training, education, horsepower, bandwidth? All the things we typically think about as capabilities to perform this seat at the level we need to perform. EOS calls this GWC (Gets it, Wants it, and has the Capacity). They might be a rock star in Ops, but a hack in Finance. Use a 5-star scale, like college athlete recruiting, where 5 stars = a perfect fit. *(5 stars = 100% fit, 4 - 80%, and so on)*
- 10 units of greatness—their own time, energy, and focus—to allocate across their current seats. For example: 2 for Integrator, 6 for Ops, 2 for Finance = 10 total units.

Then, calculate:

**Seat Impact = Units of Greatness Allocated
× Fit Factor**

Example 1: An Integrator who allocates all 10 units to a single seat—and is a 5-star fit—delivers **10 out of 10** impact in that seat. (10 x 100% = 10)

Example 2: An Ops leader who spreads their 10 units across four seats, giving just 2 to Ops... and who is only a 4-star fit (80%) for that seat... delivers **1.6 out of 10** possible impact to Ops. (2 x 80% = 1.6) That's not nearly enough!

When you tally this across your entire leadership team, the picture becomes painfully clear. You'll see which seats are dangerously underpowered and where greatness is being wasted.

A critical seat getting only *1.6 units of impact*? That's slowing you down and holding you back.

What to do with this insight:

- Coach or replace a low-fit player.
- Hire the missing piece.
- Reallocate time.
- Shift seats.
- Delegate or offload responsibilities.

Just don't ignore it.

Which leadership team seat can you afford to be weak in? None of them.

If your Integrator is the issue, your job is to see that issue clearly and fix it decisively. Or, if it's one of the other seats, take it to your Same Page Meeting to make sure your Integrator fixes it. If even one seat is weak, your leadership team is weak. You must get to the point where you can confidently say, without hesitation, "Yes. I've truly got the right people in the right seats across my entire leadership team."

One otherwise strong team had a weak Finance leader. It was apparent to everyone. This leader never completed their Rocks or hit their numbers. And guess who was at the root of most of their leadership team issues? Yep, the Finance leader. Now she was a really good person. A great core values fit. And she was trying really hard. The team saw her struggles and wanted to find a way to help. In leadership meetings, they spent more time trying to help her fix her department than they did on any other area. Extra resources were brought in, and everyone rallied around her for emotional support. It didn't work. Three quarters later, the situation had not improved. The Visionary made a change. A new Finance leader joined the team. Within the first ninety days, the problem was all fixed! The new leader sat there, totally relaxed, looking back at the rest of the team. And guess what he said: "Well, I'm all caught up. Anything else you need me to do? Or anything you need me to help you with?" The situation had flipped completely by changing that one seat. It went from being a source of friction for the team, slowing the entire train, to a boost of power, helping the train accelerate.

When your leadership team is fully aligned, it's not just that the problems go away. It's that you begin to move as one. Like a well-coordinated crew team, each leader knows their role, rows in rhythm, and pulls hard in the same direction. That's how you build speed and win the race. And when someone's out of sync? You feel the drag instantly.

Assistant

Do you have an assistant? If not, you're crazy. You need an assistant! You need somebody to help you avoid getting caught up in the "little things" that will suck you in. What's your time really worth? Have you thought about this? If you're "billable," you may already have a concrete number based on what the market pays you, which may be thousands per hour. Now consider what you are naturally great at—your Intrinsic Genius—that only you can do for your business. These activities have a huge magnitude of strategic impact. For example, you bring in a new relationship that represents a multimillion-dollar opportunity, which would have never happened without you. What's that worth to your company? And what if it didn't happen because you were busy reprogramming the phone system?

Your time (and energy) is your most valuable individual asset—period. Every moment you spend on tasks that could be handled by someone else at a fraction of your hourly value is a direct hit to your company's growth potential. Consider this: If you're a $300,000-a-year Visionary, every hour you spend on a $30-an-hour task is like burning $120 an hour in opportunity cost.

Does that seem like a mismanagement of company resources? Be careful with your time. From the perspective of the business, if you are spending time on activities that could be delegated to an effective assistant, that is a fiduciary failure. As one of my fellow EOS Implementers says, "The company needs you to act your wage!"

Delegating these activities isn't shirking responsibility; it's amplifying your impact. By offloading operational or administrative work, you free yourself to focus on the high-value activities only you can do. Things like crafting strategy, building key relationships, and driving revenue. The math is simple: invest in capable people to handle the $25-an-hour work, and you'll create exponential returns by dedicating your energy to the $500-an-hour decisions that truly move the needle. It's not just smart; it's essential for scaling your business and reclaiming your freedom.

Please get an assistant. They will not only help you, they will change your life.

If you haven't delegated work to an assistant before, you may need to intentionally develop and build that muscle. It starts by delegating one task—anything. You could start by hiring a fractional virtual assistant at less than a full-time schedule. There are excellent companies that can help you either find these people or provide them for you. Check out our Resource Page for more info and links.

VisionaryBook.com

Give them one simple task/project. That's going to cost you next to nothing. Just do it and see if it works. You may think, *Wow, this is a game changer*, and you'll realize that it's not as hard as you thought it would be. Then give them another lower-level task, and then another. In time, you'll end up giving them a whole bunch of stuff and realize just how wonderful it is to have a resource like this to help you out.

One word of caution. When I first tried that experiment myself, I set a certain level of expectation regarding how much work I'd give the assistant. And then it felt much easier than I expected. So I opened the floodgates. I pushed their limits and burned them out! I suggest discussing the "what if this work's great and I want more?" scenario with them right from the start.

Coaches and Advisors

The plural is used because you may have a rotating cast at this post. And note, there is a subtle difference between coaches and advisors.

A coach helps you grow by facilitating self-discovery and unlocking what's already inside you. Rather than giving you the answer, coaches ask powerful questions. They encourage reflection and support you in finding your own solutions. Coaching is developmental and may be ongoing. The focus may be personal or professional goals, performance improvement, or behavioral change. Coaches don't need to be subject matter experts—they're skilled in guiding your thinking and helping you find your own path.

A good analogy here is comparing you to a great athlete. Which you are, in the sport of entrepreneurship.

And we know that all great athletes have coaches. You need people around you to coach you and help ensure you're consistently bringing your A game.

One of your coaches may be your EOS Implementer, who will help coach you through the implementation of EOS. Another coach might help you with public speaking or teach you how to better manage your time. Or, you might have a coach who works with you on how to deal with conflict or other specific interpersonal issues that make you uncomfortable.

Get a coach for any areas that are important to you. They don't have to be a "forever coach." That said, you might find someone with whom you develop a nice, long relationship. As I mentioned, Dan Sullivan at Strategic Coach has been my coach for many years.

Coaches may come and go, but you'll always need at least one. You must always be growing, learning, and improving at some aspect of your role.

An advisor, on the other hand, offers expert guidance based on their experience in a specific domain. Their role is more consultative and solution-oriented, often stepping in to analyze a situation and recommend what you should do. The relationship is typically more transactional or situational, and the primary value comes from their knowledge rather than your self-discovery.

You might bring in an advisor to help you design an incentive compensation plan or assist with your intellectual property strategy. An advisor could help you with an acquisition or prepare your own company for sale. Consider any business situation you might encounter or want to pursue that exceeds your team's current experience.

In essence, a coach helps you uncover your own answers, while an advisor gives you theirs. They both can help you get there faster.

Peer Groups / Masterminds

Peer groups are composed of people with a common interest, a common experience set, or a common objective. In a solid group, there is much to learn from each other. A little bit of trust and sharing will enable the learning to flow.

Another benefit of peer groups speaks to a feeling shared by many Visionary entrepreneurs: "I'm alone." Just because you're surrounded by people doesn't mean you can talk to them about the important stuff that's on your mind. We call this the 5 percent. If you imagine a normal distribution curve ranging from bad to good, most of the stuff is in the middle, and we can talk about it with anyone. But that stuff on the tails of the distribution, both good and bad, is more problematic. If we share something bad, it may scare them off. If we share something good, they might think we're bragging. So we just keep it to ourselves. And sometimes that eats at us and leads to this feeling of isolation.

Peer groups can also develop into what might be called a "third brain." You have a whole room full of experience to tap into. You start sharing these experiences, thinking out loud, bouncing ideas off one another. Iron sharpens iron. Collaboration becomes a powerful experience. This is where the term "mastermind" comes from.

One form is a peer group organized around a specific framework of relevant training. Since the traditional education system does not adequately prepare an entrepreneur, you must fill those knowledge gaps elsewhere. For example, when we teach the 10 Pillars to a group of Visionaries, we also organize those taking the course into a Cohort of Visionaries of companies running on EOS. A few other examples of this group model are Birthing of Giants, Strategic Coach, EO's Entrepreneurial Masters Program, and Biz Owners Ed. There are also many broader peer groups available to CEOs. Some common ones that I see in the Visionary crowd are: EO, YPO, Vistage, C12, The Visionary Forum... There's actually a long, long list! Check out our Resource Page for more info and links.

VisionaryBook.com

If you aren't already in a peer group—and are interested in joining one—check out our resource list, ask your network, and bring it to our 10 Pillars Community. You may well find somebody who knows a peer group that will be great for you. Lean on them to help you fill this vital post. Joining a group can help you reach your goals faster—and hopefully with a bit less pain along the way.

Family

Your family also fills an important post. The family plays a vital role as a protective force, serving as a stabilizing shield against the noise, pressure, and distractions of the outside world. While you push boundaries and chase bold ideas, your family grounds you, reinforces your identity, and creates a safe zone where trust is unconditional and motives are pure. They help filter out opportunists, temper the chaos, and remind you of what truly matters. By anchoring your personal world with love, loyalty, and perspective, your family gives you the clarity and confidence to pursue your vision with greater focus and resilience.

Friends

Like family, great friends serve as a powerful buffer against the isolation and distortion that can come with high-stakes entrepreneurial ambition. They offer an honest perspective when others may tell you only what they think you want to hear. The best friends stand by you not for what you've built, but for who you are. In a world that often demands you show up as something other than your true self, real friends create space for authenticity, humility, and laughter. Their loyalty, candor, and shared history help keep your ego in check, your personal values intact, and your spirit energized. This makes you stronger and more grounded as you pursue your vision.

The Seven Forces

Now that you have the right people manning each post in your shield wall, let's discuss seven special forces, which the right people will help generate for you. These forces will serve as your "tailwind," driving you forward, into the headwinds you will face while pursuing your vision.

The inspiration for these Seven Forces goes back to something I learned from Gino years ago that he called "Seven Special People." He learned it from one of his friends, Vinnie Romano, during a deep conversation they were having one day. I've chosen to focus on the "forces" these people provide so as not to confuse you with more "people" beyond the Seven Posts we've just discussed. You'll find many of these will come from people filling your Seven Posts.

While one person will not provide all of these forces for you, they may well provide more than one. And for some forces, you may have to look for more than one person to help you. Regardless, you will benefit from having each of these provided by at least one person to guide and propel you:

1. **Intercession:** Stepping in and advocating on your behalf.

2. **Mentorship**: Sharing wisdom and knowledge from their experience.

3. **Challenge:** Pushing you out of your comfort zone to grow.

4. **Confrontation:** Telling you the hard truths you need to hear.

5. **Encouragement:** Building your confidence and self-belief.

6. **Partnership:** Walking with you, side-by-side, through the journey.

7. **Rescue:** Stepping in when you need to be rescued or redirected.

THE 7 FORCES

RESCUE PARTNERSHIP ENCOURAGEMENT CONFRONTATION CHALLENGE MENTORSHIP INTERCESSION

—MCW

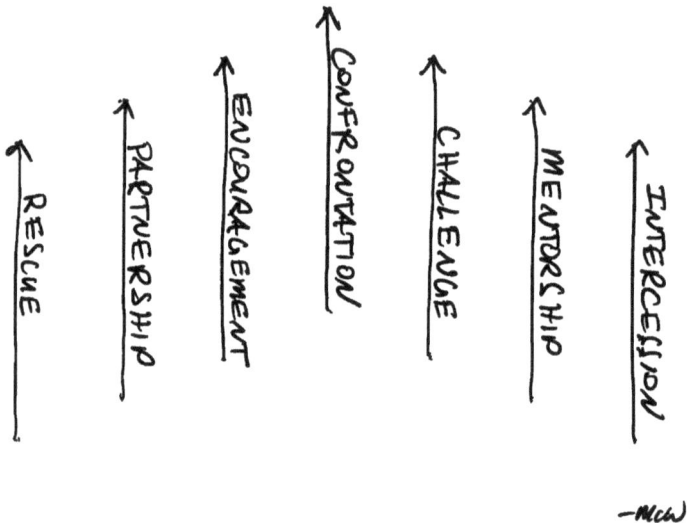

Intercession. This is the person who came to your side when you were getting backed into a corner on the playground by somebody three times bigger than you. They're five times bigger than you, and they backed that one bully off. They're the intercessor. They're the one who stands up for you.

Mentorship. A mentor is somebody who's teaching and guiding you, like Sam Cupp was for Gino. Like Gino has done for me. They're bringing you along, providing coaching, counseling, listening, training, and teaching you. Throughout your life's journey, different mentors may come alongside you. As the saying goes, "When the student is ready, the teacher appears." Who has been your greatest mentor to date? Do you have more than one mentor today?

Challenge. The challenger hears an idea you have and tries to push the goal out even a little further than you had initially intended. They get you to think more about it, to push yourself. You might not always choose to do what they suggest, but the point is that they are always pushing you beyond your current dreams.

Confrontation. Everyone needs to have a Confronter. A confronter keeps you from kidding yourself. Sometimes we tell so many people a thing that we actually start to believe it's true, and then we get lost. Sometimes the people around you won't tell you the truth. This is a common reality in your world as a Visionary. People can be afraid of you and often find themselves saying yes to please you. You need somebody who will say, "No, that's wrong...that's not real...that's not true." The confronter keeps you honest with yourself.

Encouragement. You will definitely need an Encourager for when things get tough. Because, guess what? They will! Being a Visionary gets painfully difficult at times. Your Encourager gives you strength to persevere, sustain, and carry you through.

Partnership. A partner is somebody to share your wins and losses with. In my EO forum, a peer group I mentioned earlier, we talked about the 5 percent. Let's think about the distribution curve of all the "stuff."

We've got good stuff on one end and bad stuff on the other. We can talk to a lot of people about all this stuff in the middle. The middle stuff is easy. And yet we all have stuff on the far ends of the curve too. Stuff so good it feels like bragging. Or so bad it might scare them away. You end up keeping that stuff inside—and that's not healthy. It'll eat away at you. That's the stuff you tell your partner.

When we win big, they're just as happy for us as we are. And when we have a loss, they listen to and support us. Everyone needs a partner in their corner.

Rescue. Right before you run off a cliff—or take that self-damaging step that cannot be undone—who steps in to stop you? To save you from yourself? The Rescuer. They help you see what you've gotten too close to realize the danger. Or maybe you are just too naïve in this area to know better in the first place. The Rescuer stops you from doing further damage and helps you get back to pointing in the right direction.

As you think of these Seven Forces, please keep in mind that many of them may come from people outside your business: Coaches, Advisors, Peer Groups, Family, and Friends. While their guidance may well help with your company, the advice will also permeate areas of your life that extend well beyond.

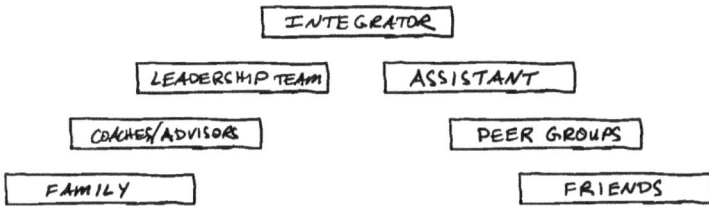

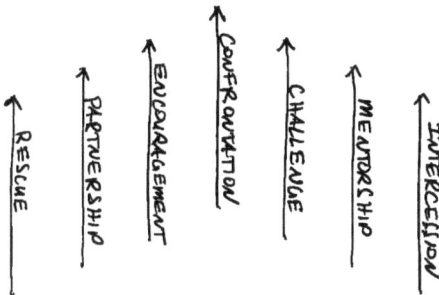

So how solid is your shield wall? Where are the gaps? And what would it mean for your future if you filled them with real strength?

Surround yourself well because your greatness depends on it.

Transformation

AREA	RANK	WHO?	PERFORMANCE
7 POSTS			
INTEGRATOR			
LEADERSHIP TEAM			
ASSISTANT			
COACHES / ADVISORS			
PEER GROUPS			
FAMILY			
FRIENDS			
7 FORCES			
INTERCESSION			
MENTORSHIP			
CHALLENGE			
CONFRONTATION			
ENCOURAGEMENT			
PARTNERSHIP			
RESCUE			

Before you take a few quiet minutes to complete this exercise, let me set it up for you. You'll notice a complete list of the Seven Posts and the Seven Forces.

First, next to the list is a column titled "Rank." I want you to rank them in order of importance in your life. Don't overthink this. The top-ranked ones should come to mind quickly, as will the bottom-ranked ones. And feel free to work it from both ends: rank a few at the top, then a few at the bottom. Go back and forth until you get through them all. And don't spend any time trying to decide between the ones in the middle; it won't matter much which one ends up at number 4 vs. number 5.

Next, write the names of the people who are either currently filling that role for you or who you could see filling that role in the future. For example, you may already have someone in mind that you'd like to some-day fill the challenge or mentorship force for you. They may not be filling that role for you now, but they are your target for the future. It's somebody you might go after with intent.

Finally, the last column in this exercise is about Performance. How well are you doing right now with each? The scale is 1–10, with 10 being best. Ten means it's rolling, it's going great. One means it's not there, it's vacant.

Now, reflect on how you ranked them and how well you're doing with each. As you reflect on what you jotted down, pick out your top three biggest gaps to improve. Take five quiet minutes and complete this exercise, making sure to highlight any areas you'd like to discuss in the Community.

Pillar 3: Surround Yourself

- ☐ Has filled each of the Seven Posts effectively and is confident that all are performing well.
- ☐ Quickly addresses any gaps that may develop in the Seven Posts.
- ☐ Has identified the Seven Forces—the vital human relationships in their world—and can name at least one person for each.
- ☐ Invests intentionally in each Seven Forces relationship, building trust, rhythm, and clarity.
- ☐ Has built a solid "shield wall" to effectively protect them from unexpected chaos and external threats.

To round out this pillar, review your Visionary Report Card (VRC). Read the mindsets above that go along with Pillar 3. Give yourself Xs or slashes next to the mindsets you're doing well in, leaving blank the mindsets where you have substantial work to do. Then give yourself a rating on how well you are doing overall. Again, the scale is 1–10, with 10 being the highest.

Up next is Pillar 4: Commit to Your Operating System.

PILLAR 4
COMMIT TO YOUR OPERATING SYSTEM

Discipline equals freedom.

—Jocko Willink

Outside of technology, the term operating system (OS) is used metaphorically to describe a set of core rules, tools, structures, and processes that drive how something functions and makes decisions—whether it's a business, a team, or an individual.

For you, a visionary entrepreneur, an operating system is what transforms your raw ambition into repeatable results. That infrastructure keeps everything focused, aligned, moving forward, and under control, even as your vision expands. Whether it's a business operating system for growing your business, an individual operating system for managing your personal energy and focus, or a more specific system tailored to one of the more unique elements of your ecosystem, they all share a few key traits:

- **Clarity:** Define what matters most and why
- **Structure:** Provide consistent rhythms, roles, and rules
- **Alignment:** Ensure everyone (or everything) moves in the same direction
- **Accountability:** Track performance and progress against goals
- **Simplicity:** Strip away noise to focus on what works

An operating system is the structured way you bring your vision to life. It's the underlying framework that channels your big ideas into real-world action. Your OS aligns people, processes, and priorities so your business (or life) can run with focus, consistency, and momentum. It's the difference between trying to fly by instinct alone, a.k.a. "by the seat of your pants," or having a flight plan, a crew, and a dashboard that gets you where you're meant to go.

> An operating system is the structured way you bring your vision to life.

Increase Your Odds of Success

As you operate within any Operating System, there are three things you can do that will collectively increase your odds of success:

1. **Choose *one*.** While you may employ multiple operating systems in your world, make sure you don't have more than one for the same thing. And recognize there may be more than one good option to choose from. In fact, there probably are! Your job is to not fall into the trap of mixing and matching, taking some pieces from this one and some from that one. That "mix & match" approach has proven to create more complexity and confusion for everyone involved, and has shown no real upside.

2. **Don't waffle.** Once you've chosen the right OS, lean into it fully. It's counterproductive when your actions don't match your words. You tell everyone we're going to use a certain OS, then you repeatedly seem to violate whatever structure that involves. As you can imagine, this is very frustrating for your people. They never know what to expect. And they're unlikely to fully commit themselves, because they have some expectation that you might pull the plug on the whole OS at any moment. Instead, be a role model for them. Embrace the structure as designed. Let them see you doing so. This will inspire them to get fully onboard with the OS—right alongside you.

3. **Work toward Mastery.** Recognize that the learning is never done. As you initially implement an OS and begin to use it, the learning begins. Some things come easily for you, while others are more difficult. Each individual, each organization, is different in this regard. The more you use it, the better you get. You train

the others involved and those who join in the future. You also learn things from others who use the OS. Maybe they figured out something that you had missed. And maybe you teach them something as well. You get confident. And then you drift…the training gets rushed or maybe skipped altogether. Changes emerge accidentally, not because you intended to make them. It's like the old "telephone game." At the end of the chain, the original message has transformed into something that is now unrecognizable. This can happen with your OS. Striving for mastery is how we counteract this ever-present force of resistance. Always learning, training, teaching, coaching, sharing, and recalibrating ourselves with the original design of the OS—a proven approach that you know works.

Climb the Operating System Ladder

As an entrepreneurial Visionary, when you think about an operating system (OS), I want you to think about four specific types. These types are organized in a sequence, beginning with your individual perspective, then expanding to your overall perspective on the business.

In short:

1. **Individual OS:** What do you want to be uniquely true in the key areas of your life?

2. **Visionary OS:** How can you maximize your effectiveness in this role?

3. **V/I Duo OS™:** How can you maximize the power of your V/I Duo relationship?

4. **Business OS:** How can you harness and focus the human energy in your business for maximum impact?

THE OS LADDER

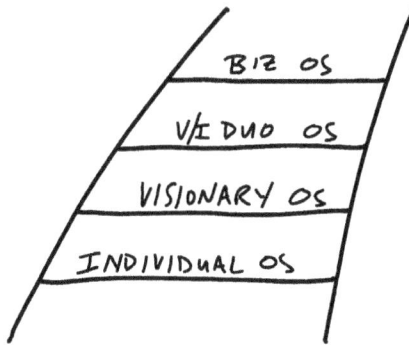

— mcw

Now, let's dive deeper into each one to help you better understand what you'll really need.

Individual OS

First is the operating system for you, as the human, who also happens to be an entrepreneurial Visionary. You need a program to help you hone in on what's truly most important to you as an individual.

Clarity enables the alignment and integration of your business and personal worlds. How do they come together? How do they affect each other? How do we keep them from working at odds with one another? Absent this clarity, it becomes increasingly difficult to know where you should focus. You end up spending your finite time, energy, and resources on projects that don't really move you closer to your goals. In fact, you may be doing things that move you forward in one sense, while moving you backward in another! The sooner you create this clarity and make it all visible, the sooner you'll make progress in the right direction.

I have developed a framework to facilitate the thought process required to get you there. This system is broken down into what I call the 9 Domains of Freedom. These nine make up the Exponential Freedom model. You've already touched on some of them back in Pillar 2. Those three form the Foundation Layer of the model. We further build on those with a Multiplier Layer, and finally, an Impact Layer. This is where all that you bring to this world, amplified by those multipliers, finally comes into focus to deliver the impact you care about most.

Rather than expanding further on the model in this chapter, I've included it in our online Resource page, and it will provide an important next step in your journey.

VisionaryBook.com

Everything is all there. I look forward to hearing what you think!

Visionary OS

Next, you need an OS for operating effectively in your role as an entrepreneurial Visionary. This OS advances you from understanding what you really want as an individual to understanding how you channel that into a specific role where you interact with others. This role is unique in the world and completely different from any other role in an entrepreneurial organization. The stakes involved could not be higher. The livelihood and ultimate success of your business are in play, along with the livelihood of all the people in the company.

As you might have already gathered, preparing you for the Visionary role is the core focus of this book. Master these 10 Pillars, and you'll be on the right path for what is required to be truly great as an entrepreneurial Visionary.

V/I Duo OS

Next, you need an operating system for your Visionary/ Integrator Duo relationship. This is why the book *Rocket Fuel* exists. In addition to teaching the roles, our focus in writing that book was on trying to build a system and structure to help raise this relationship from one that is naturally combative (and filled with friction and dysfunction) and turn it into a powerful synergy. That sort of relationship will propel your business to the next level of success.

Gino and I call this V/I Duo operating system "The Five Rules":

1. Stay on the Same Page.
2. No End Runs.
3. The Integrator Is the Tie-Breaker.
4. Owner/Employee Rules of the Game.
5. Maintain Mutual Respect.

Let's quickly walk through each of them to unpack what they really mean for you.

Rule #1: Stay on the Same Page. This rule is number one for a reason. When we ask Visionaries and Integrators what they struggle with the most, staying on the same page is the most common answer. They often think that because they spend a lot of time together, they're going to end up on the same page. That's simply *not* how it works.

Just because you have offices right next to each other, see each other in the hall all the time, or hang out on the weekends, doesn't mean you talk about the issues you need to discuss. Those hit-and-run interactions tend to be very surface-level. They don't really get down deep into the meaty stuff. So that's where the Same Page Meeting tool comes into play.

A healthy Visionary/Integrator Duo should have a Same Page Meeting at least once a month. If the two of you are ever not on the same page, you or your Integrator—or your leadership team—will feel tension as a result. If so, you'll want to increase the frequency of these Same Page Meetings to every two weeks, or maybe even once a week, until you can get back on the same page and consistently stay there.

If your V/I Duo relationship is brand-new, weekly might be the perfect place to start.

Be sure to block two to four hours for the Same Page Meeting. You want to go in with the mindset: "We're going to lock the door and stay in there until we get every issue squared away. We will not walk out of that meeting without being a hundred percent on the same page about any problem that's going to influence the company after we leave here." As long as it takes. Sometimes it's going to take longer (4+ hours), and that's all right.

Follow the same agenda every time. Start with a check-in. This check-in is different from the check-in you do with the other leaders in a weekly leadership team meeting. It's deeper and reflective of the depth of the relationship that you want to have with your Integrator. As I've mentioned, some of my clients have referred to this V/I relationship as their "business spouse," so let's treat it like that.

You're digging deeper and asking questions like, "What's really going on? Where's your head at? What's happening in your world?" Remember when we talked about Partnership as one of the Seven Special Forces? Well, this is someone you can share your wins and losses with. Expect to hear some of that from them as well. You'll hear some really great updates—and some awful ones too. You need to know where they're at and how they're feeling, and they need to know the same about you.

Next, build the Issues List. Your Integrator might have been keeping track of them all along and is ready to get their issues on the list. Or you may both come in with nothing specific in mind, and as you sit down, ideas begin popping out. Start by reading aloud any issues left over from last time. Then add whatever you brought that you prepared beforehand, as well as anything else that comes to mind as you begin to focus. Get all of your worries and concerns onto the issues list, where they all become top of mind again.

Now that you both understand what issues are in front of you, prioritize your top three, and begin to solve them. Look for the number one item on the list that is the most impactful for your company to knock out, solve, and eliminate forever. That should always be your first item. Some Duos have one person pick their first three issues, and then the next person picks their next three, and so on until you've made your way through the list. Gino and I used to simply take turns as we made our way through our issues list. You pick one, then I pick one. There are different paths to work through the issues, and all are fine. As long as you are dedicated to addressing the most impactful ones first, you're good.

An important reason to stay on the same page is for your leadership team. If you don't, you're punishing them, and it's not their fault. Have you ever been in a leadership team meeting where the other leaders watch you two go back and forth? Their heads move side-to-side as this V/I Ping Pong match unfolds before them. Recognize how painful this is for the other leaders on the team.

One of you needs to recognize what is happening and say, "Time out. We're not on the same page. We need to kick this back to our Same Page Meeting. We'll get aligned there first, and then we'll bring it back here to the leadership team." Sometimes you'll have a great leader on your leadership team who's strong enough to speak up and suggest that the two of you take it back to your Same Page Meeting, but please don't rely on that. Police yourself.

One V/I Duo, John and Sam, somehow misunderstood the Same Page Meeting the first time around. And it was apparent in their quarterly meetings. The team repeatedly had to stop so the two of them could catch up and get aligned. This process consumed much of the team's time together and their energy. It was equally frustrating for everyone else. When John and Sam realized that they'd mistaken surface-level "daily contact" with the depth of the Same Page discipline, they recommitted to do it right. The impact was immediate. Quarterly meetings became much more focused and productive now that the two of them were already consistently aligned on the majority of items to be discussed.

As you're reading this book, take the opportunity to identify items that need to go on your Same Page issues list. Write them all down so that when you go to your next Same Page Meeting, you'll have those issues ready to talk about.

Rule #2: No End Runs. What does an end run look like? Allow me to describe two scenarios for you.

Scenario 1:
Someone in the organization says, "I've been going to Jane (the Visionary) for all my problems since I've been at this company. This new issue just came up, and

I'm going to talk to Jane." That person walks through the office, right past the Integrator, and straight into Jane's office. If Jane hasn't been trained on End Runs yet, Jane's probably going to do the same thing she's been doing all along. Which is, handle it.

Then, as the person marches back out, right past the new Integrator. That Integrator's left sitting there, head spinning and wondering, "What just happened?" It's very difficult, if not impossible, for them to be effective in that situation.

Scenario 2:

A Visionary is sitting around one day, and a thought passes through their brain. And what do you think they do? They go out into the organization, or pick up the phone, or grab somebody a level or two below the Integrator and say, "Hey, you need to do this!" They make the call and give that person a new direction about what they should do. Or, they've been wanting to make a decision, and they go off on their own, do it, and leave their Integrator with their head spinning (again), wondering what just happened.

I refer to this second scenario as "tampering."

NO END RUNS

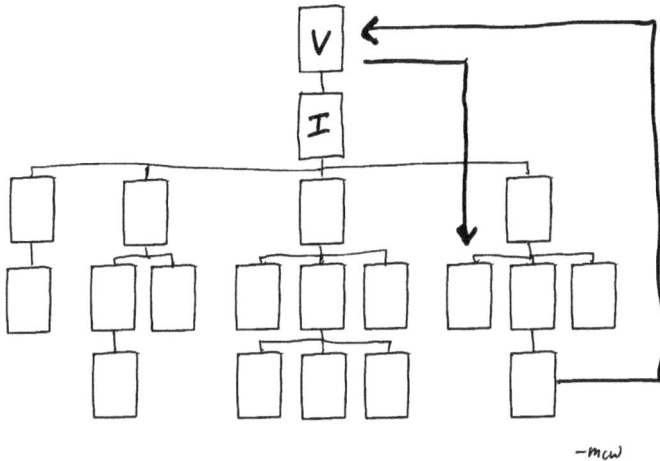

—mcw

Remember, the rule is "No End Runs."

When the tampering urge begins to build, a Visionary must resist it. Don't put an initiative in motion that wasn't discussed. We want communication to flow freely across the Accountability Chart. Side to side and top to bottom. Communication is encouraged. Go talk to people! You just need to stop short of making decisions or giving direction in the field. Let that happen through your intentional structure of accountability. You designed it that way for a reason.

Likewise, when someone comes into your office and asks you to make a decision for them or asks you to tell them what to do. In these cases, you must employ what we call "The Question":

"Are you going to tell the Integrator, or am I going to tell the Integrator?"

Because one of you needs to tell the Integrator.

117

Within thirty days of implementing The Question, you will drive end runs out of your organization. They'll stop because it gets uncomfortable. The person walks into your office thinking, "I know how to work you. The Integrator? Not so much." When you hit them with the question, they realize they have to deal with it the right way. They learn, and eventually, they stop.

A Visionary named Tom had built his company from the ground up. But like many visionaries, Tom had a habit of doing "end runs." He'd bypass his Integrator, Sarah, and go directly to team members to give instructions or make decisions. It wasn't malicious. He just thought he was being efficient.

One day, Tom noticed a dip in sales and decided to jump in. Without consulting Sarah, he went straight to the sales team and told them to change their approach. The team, eager to please the boss, implemented Tom's changes immediately.

What Tom didn't realize was that Sarah had already been working on a carefully planned strategy to address the sales issue. Her plan was based on data, team input, and a clear understanding of the company's long-term goals. When Tom's changes clashed with Sarah's strategy, it created confusion and frustration. The sales team didn't know whose direction to follow, and productivity plummeted even further.

At their next Same Page Meeting, Sarah called it out. She showed Tom how his end run had undercut her role and thrown the team off. It was a hard conversation. And a turning point. Tom realized he wasn't just stepping on toes. He was weakening that structure he'd worked so hard to build.

From that day forward, Tom committed to the "no end runs" rule. He and Sarah doubled down on their Same Page Meetings to ensure they were aligned. Tom learned to trust Sarah to execute the vision, and the company thrived as a result.

Rule #3: The Integrator Is the Tiebreaker. For some Visionaries, it's hard to understand why we teach this rule. To help you understand, consider this. If done properly, you and the Integrator are inhabiting two halves of the same brain because of the Same Page Meeting discipline. If you're discussing and exploring the key issues, you will walk out of that Same Page Meeting completely aligned. Your Integrator will be in a great position to make a decision on whatever question is brought to them. Your perspective should already be baked into their thinking. If they're unsure you're fully aligned—and it's a big decision—they'll circle back with you before pulling the trigger.

You may be thinking that you possess that knowledge too, so why the Integrator? Well, they also know all the details on the ground, details you're likely not close enough to see. They know what jobs are in place, what projects are underway, and where resources are constrained. They know when a person is under a tremendous amount of stress. A great Integrator has their ear to the ground, and it puts them in a better position to break the tie. Always in the context of your shared vision and the greater good.

Now, how often is there actually a tie to break? Rarely.

In my experience, at least 90 percent of the time, when the leadership team is working through an issue, they naturally reach a conclusion. And that's not because they vote. This is not a democracy. In fact, if consensus does happen, that's merely a happy accident. We need decisions. Made by leaders. With accountability.

This requires that we have true "leaders" on the leadership team. When leaders who make decisions have the right input, they're willing to be held accountable for getting it right. If we make those decisions for them, who's accountable? Nobody. Or it's just back on us again. To paraphrase a story I heard from Patrick Lencioni, "If you need me to make your decision for you, then one of us isn't needed here."

The Leader/Doer Evolver[IP]

To lead effectively, every member of the leadership team must evolve in how they allocate their energy. I call this the *Leader/Doer Evolver*.

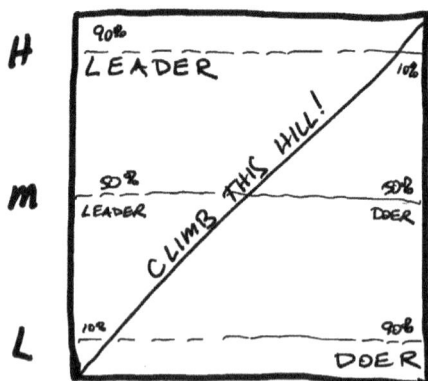

Early on, most leaders spend the majority of their time as *doers*. Cranking out deliverables, reacting to problems, staying buried in the day-to-day. That's production.

But true leadership requires a shift.

They must graduate from doer to leader—investing time and energy into:

- **LMA** (Leadership, Management, and creating Accountability)
- **Making decisions** (instead of "kicking the can" or overdelegating upward)
- **Creating capacity** (through process, tools, automation, structure, or clarity, not just hiring more people)
- **Getting stuff done through others** (not doing it all themselves)

It's a progression. If they can't LMA, they can't lead. If they can't make clear decisions, they'll bottleneck the team. If they don't create capacity, they'll remain underwater. And if they can't delegate to elevate, they'll never scale. And you'll stay right where you are.

When I first meet a leadership team, most members are operating 90 percent as doers and only 10 percent as leaders. But the best teams I've worked with flip that ratio—spending 90 percent or more of their energy leading.

This is not unlike what Stephen Covey referred to as the P/PC (Production and Production Capacity) Balance. *Production* is the output, the work, the results. *Production Capacity* is your ability to keep delivering that output, and even more, over time. Covey's P/PC Balance is a reminder: if you only focus on production, you burn out the engine. Production gets you today's win. Production Capacity ensures you can keep winning. It's about building the machine, not just running it hard.

That evolution unlocks everything.

Once you build the structure, solve the people issues, and learn to create capacity, you get a team that stops playing defense. They stop protecting their "full plates" and start engaging energetically in solving what matters most. That's when the fun really starts.

However, a team can still sometimes get stuck. If one leader says, "We need to do this," and another says, "We need to do that," there's no clear decision, and the team lacks direction. Maybe the decision will impact multiple areas, and the leaders will start arguing to pursue different paths. For example, marketing is pushing to go in one direction, and finance is pushing to go in another. They try to work it out, and they just can't. So they get stuck.

You can't stay stuck. If you stay stuck, you can die.

You must make decisions and move forward. When the leadership team can't, the Integrator steps in. They are on the same page with you. They have your shared vision and shared priorities. They are armed with all of this context to help them make the best call.

Then, given all of those inputs, they make that call.

Now, what happens if they screw up? It happens. When it does, they fail fast and learn from it. There's coaching and growth that happens, just like for anybody. The first time that you were put in a position to make a decision (when you were a young manager or when you were a young entrepreneur), you didn't always make the right decision. Nobody does. We want to allow for learning from those mistakes, particularly on the issues that aren't capable of sinking our ship.

We need to lean into our Integrator. Trust them. Take the time to prepare them to make the right call, then let them do it!

Imagine a leadership team debating whether to launch a new product. The Visionary is fired up about the idea: It's bold, exciting, and could disrupt the market. But the team is split. Some leaders are concerned about timing, resource constraints, and potential risks. The discussion drags on, emotions rise, and no consensus emerges.

This is where the Integrator steps in. Their role is to cut through the noise, weigh the facts, and make the final call. They're the tiebreaker, ensuring the decision aligns with the company's priorities and capacity. Without the Integrator, the team could stay stuck in endless debate, delaying action and progress. The Integrator's ability to make the tough call keeps the organization moving forward with clarity and focus.

Should you ever step in? When should your decision trump that of your Integrator? In a few rare instances, this is the case. And hopefully these get sorted in your Same Page Meeting as part of their development process. First, if your Integrator is not yet comfortable with a particular decision, it may be because it is outside their experience set. They haven't had time yet to fully learn whatever they need to feel confident in their role. Second, if an urgent situation arises—one that could sink the ship—and your Integrator isn't ready to make that major decision. Maybe they are new in the company, but this decision can't wait. Finally, if the Integrator shows a pattern of bad decisions, despite your best coaching, you might have the wrong Integrator. You may need to make a change and fire them from the seat.

Rule #4: Owner/EE Rules of the Game. You are an Employee when you are working "in" the business.

Are you an Owner of your business? Do you have Partners? Do you know what rights come with being an owner of your business? Well, it might surprise you to learn that "ownership" fundamentally comes with only two rights. First, you have the right to your share of the profits. Second, you have a right to stay informed and have your say in the major decisions of the business. And when it comes to the "major decisions," these are the biggies:

- Are we going to take on debt?
- Are we going to take on another equity shareholder? Or buy one out?
- Are we going to make an acquisition?
- Are we going to sell our office building?
- Are we going to sell the company?

We're talking about that level of big decisions—maybe the top 5 percent. These updates and decisions are discussed in a forum we call the "Owners' Box." I'll talk more about that in a moment.

Outside the Owners' Box, the other 95 percent of the decisions fall to your Visionary/Integrator Duo, and the rest of the leadership team, to execute whatever the Owners have decided is important. Whatever the overall charter is for this business. Whether it is to maximize growth and revenue, maximize profit, maximize the valuation of the business, and so on. That dictates the high-level direction that you want to pursue. The leadership team is then charged with figuring out how to make it happen and executing that plan. As Owners, you hold them accountable for that, starting with the V/I Duo.

Maybe you noticed that I did not say an Owner has the right to be an employee in the business. Does that surprise you? By way of analogy, if you own an NFL team, should you have the right to play quarterback? Or be the General Manager? Of course not! Ownership alone does not give you that right.

If an Owner does take a seat in the Accountability Chart as an employee, it's essential that they are truly the best person to fill the seat. Just like we expect from anyone else in the company. Sometimes, an Owner is the best person to fill a seat on the leadership team. And sometimes they are our best option to fill a seat that falls somewhere below the leadership team. Both of these scenarios are common.

Any Owners who fill those seats, serving as employees in the business, must agree to live by these five rules:

1. Owners always form a united front in the presence of others.

2. Owners agree to let the Integrator make those tie-breaker decisions "in" the business.

3. Owners don't engage in politics, pull rank, or make end runs.

4. Owners don't talk trash behind people's backs.

5. Owners have complete accountability for the role or seat that we're sitting in.

You must be a role model for what you would expect of any other employee hired. If you play the "owner card" of privilege and say something to the effect of "That doesn't apply to me, because I'm an Owner," that's when the whole system begins to come unwound. Your words no longer have integrity. It's like the parent who says, "Do as I say, not as I do." In that case, you're not modeling the behavior that you're asking from everybody else. People sense that. And it undercuts the integrity of the entire system. It makes it very difficult for people to buy in.

Owners must play by the same rules. As Owners go, so goes the rest of the business.

One essential discipline in support of this Rule is what we call the "Owners' Box" Meeting. I want you to picture the Owners' Box as a related structure that floats above the top of the Accountability Chart. If you are an Owner, you automatically have a place there. Even if you are not an employee. The Visionary is almost always an Owner, and sometimes the Integrator is as well. This group should meet monthly, and at least one meeting each quarter should do a deep dive into the financials of the business.

In this meeting, Owners are encouraged to discuss whatever is necessary to help them get and stay aligned. If you have unanswered questions, this is the place to ask them. If you have concerns, this is the place to air them. The Visionary and Integrator might provide an update. You might occasionally bring in certain people from the leadership team to speak to a specific issue or update the Owners on a key initiative. It's all fair game to discuss. For any high-level decisions you make, update the leadership team so they can adjust their plans accordingly. But any unresolved differences must stay there. They cannot leave that room. You must address the organization as a united front.

As Owners, we all commit to certain healthy behaviors in our Owner role:

- We commit to participating in the owner meeting. Attending and engaging in the discussion. Staying informed by following communications and asking questions.
- Straight-line communication is essential. No being vague. Say what you mean. That gives us a chance to deal with it. And don't spin it. Just say it. Rip off the bandage, and let's get into it.
- 50/50 dialogue is the standard. Owners should listen to each other. No single person should be dominating the airwaves. On average, the speaking/listening should be balanced around the room. If someone needs to listen more, or someone else needs to speak up, call it out. Make it visible. And get everyone engaged.
- Owners must present a united front "in" the business. You can talk about anything and everything in the Owners' Box; this is the place to really let it fly. Yet even if you get sideways with each other in the meeting, you must walk out of the room locked arm-in-arm. This is how your employees will see their ownership team.
- When issues are unresolved, you must leave them in that Owners' Box room until they get resolved. We must not bring any of that "dirty laundry" into the business. Remind yourself

that you'll return to the Owners' Box soon enough and get another chance to solve that issue for good.

Finally, a few words about compensation. I urge you to separate Owner compensation from Employee compensation. When these two are blended, it almost always creates confusion and quite often a sense of entitlement. Any Owner compensation should be structured from the perspective that each Owner is only sitting in the Owners' Box. That's it. It contemplates no further involvement in the day-to-day of the business. If that were the case, here's what we agree would be fair and in accordance with our Operating Agreement. If an Owner also sits in an Employee seat, the compensation for that seat should be calculated from the perspective of any outside hire sitting in the seat—based on performance expectations and qualifications.

Simply put, do not compensate an Owner's employee role any differently than you would a similarly qualified outsider sitting in the same seat. If you adhere to these two simple guidelines, you'll protect yourself from a great deal of owner confusion, entitlement, and hard feelings. And perhaps most of all, a sense of resentment from your other employees.

Rule #5: Maintain Mutual Respect. Friction and tension between Visionaries and Integrators are both normal and healthy because you are wired differently. That's the whole idea because you also have very different roles. In fact, it's this polarity that helps make the relationship—this V/I Duo combination—as powerful as it is.

Despite these differences, you must never make a negative comment about your counterpart to anyone else in the organization...ever.

If you go around complaining about your Integrator, you're killing them. You're cutting them off at the knees.

You must maintain mutual respect.

Keep in mind that your V/I Duo should be an eye-level relationship. The Integrator is not your minion. They're not somebody that you look down on. You want somebody you can respect, trust, and believe in enough that you can function as true partners and collaborators.

For their part, they must be strong enough that when you lean into them, they lean back into you—appropriately. They're not pushing back in a disrespectful way. Sometimes opposition is necessary so you can move forward.

Some of you entrepreneurial Visionaries burn pretty bright. You're intense. You're overpowering. And not everyone can handle that. I've seen many Integrators get "melted" by the intensity of their Visionary. And I'm not asking you to turn that intensity down. You must be yourself. Yet you must also find an Integrator that has the appropriate level of "asbestos coating" to be able to stand right beside your flame without getting burned, never shrinking from the light. The Integrator speaks truth to your power and makes sure you hear the things you need to hear.

That is the Integrator you will respect.

Make sure you treat them right. Show them their due respect.

If you don't, it may cost you a great Integrator. During our research for *Rocket Fuel*, Gino and I discovered a sizable disparity between who was naturally wired to be a Visionary, as opposed to an Integrator—roughly a 4:1 ratio. Making things worse, that one Integrator was not a great match for all four Visionaries. Maybe they were only a good fit for one or two of them. From this information, the Integrator clearly emerged as a scarce commodity in the *Rocket Fuel* equation.

In other words, we saw a shortage of people who were truly wired to be an Integrator. And of those who were wired to be Integrators, many of them were not even aware yet. We could create value by helping Integrators identify themselves and further develop to become truly great in that role. In essence, we built the Rocket Fuel Academy as a training "factory" to prepare more great Integrators, and then help match them up with great Visionaries.

Remember, they are a scarce and valuable commodity in the world. And if you mistreat them, they may well leave you.

I teach Integrators who find themselves frustrated in a dysfunctional V/I Duo that they always have three choices:

1. Stop complaining about it, and just tolerate it.
2. Confront it, and have the hard conversation needed to change it.
3. Leave it. Move on. Life's too short.

Are you treating your Integrator with mutual respect? If not, you may be driving them towards these three choices. You may be driving them to leave you. And, if they're good, other Visionaries are literally circling the waters to find them. Bottom line, if you have a great

Integrator, treating them with respect is not only the right thing to do, it's also one of your most powerful retention strategies.

Let me be clear about what real mutual respect looks like in the V/I Duo: It's authentic. It's built on trust, not ego. Like any great partnership—or marriage—the duo is rooted in vulnerability, strength, and shared belief in each other's value.

Neither partner is made to feel "less than." You give each other the benefit of the doubt. You address issues privately, never publicly. And here's the hard rule: You never make a negative comment about your counterpart to anyone else in the organization. Ever.

Yes, there's friction. That's not a problem; it's part of the magic. Every Visionary/Integrator Duo has tension. That's the polarity that powers Rocket Fuel.

Tension and mutual respect are not opposites. They can, and must, coexist. The Five Rules give you the structure to harness that tension and convert it into focused power.

The Benefits of Mutual Respect

1. **For the Integrator**
   - They experience a healthy partnership, not a "minion" dynamic.
   - They're empowered to make decisions and practice their craft without fear.
   - They gain clarity, autonomy, and purpose in their role.

2. **For the Visionary**

- Your relationship holds the Integrator accountable in a *functional* way.
- Your creativity is freed up. No more bottlenecks or overload.
- You feel *seen*, connected, and actively contributing. Not pushed out to pasture.

3. **For the Leadership Team**

- The V/I Duo becomes a model of trust, openness, and healthy communication.
- When mutual respect is present, it's obvious. And so is the lack of it.
- The team's belief in the V/I structure and in each other rises dramatically.

4. **For the Entire Organization**

- A healthy V/I Duo sets the tone for the whole company.
- People follow your duo's lead. Especially in how conflict and power are handled.
- Ultimately, mutual respect between Visionary and Integrator is foundational to living The EOS Life®.

So, what to do when mutual respect is lacking? If the respect begins to erode—even slightly—it must be addressed quickly. Here's how:

- Use your Same Page Meetings. Talk it through. Get back to alignment.

- Show up equally strong. You don't have to match *style*, but you do need to match *strength*.
- Remember: either person has the right—and the responsibility—to take the lead in addressing the gap.

If you can't get there? You're back to the three choices:

1. Tolerate it.
2. Confront it.
3. Leave it.

And don't kid yourself. Your team can feel it. When respect is missing, employees may start to exploit the cracks in your relationship. They'll use the dysfunction as leverage, often unconsciously, to avoid accountability, manipulate outcomes, or advance personal agendas.

Don't give them that opening.

Stanley was a talented Visionary for a financial services company. Brilliant. Prolific. So many ideas. Never met a problem he couldn't solve. Julie was his Integrator and strong in her own right. However, the relationship wasn't right. Every challenge Julie raised was consistently met with Stanley's reflex response of "Oh, I've already solved that." Yet, digging a bit further, it became apparent that the solutions mostly existed in Stanley's head. But there were no documents. No process. Nothing tangible to go along with what existed in his mind. Stanley became frustrated and felt Julie simply wasn't smart enough to read his mind. His frustration evolved into dismissiveness. He took away aspects of Julie's job and cut her out of conversations, which was increasingly painful for her. The team also shared her pain.

Julie confronted the situation (choice #2) repeatedly with Stanley, and he'd commit to slow down a bit and not always jump to conclusions. But he wouldn't stick to the agreement. He'd soon revert to the same old instinctive patterns. After a while, Julie made choice #3 and she moved on to another Visionary, where their V/I Duo flourished. Stanley struggled to find a replacement. Turnover accelerated in his team. He couldn't do it all by himself. And eventually, he lost the company entirely.

Of course, we all have these three choices in life. And, on the other hand, you may be the one facing this choice right now. Maybe you have an Integrator that just isn't getting the job done. If so, which option will you choose? I surely hope it's not #1.

Business OS

Finally, to help you get more of what you want from your business, you will need a business operating system. Today, there are literally dozens of these available in the marketplace. Unfortunately, many of them use language that all sounds very similar. This will make your selection process even more challenging. As an entrepreneurial Visionary, regardless of which Business OS you choose, make sure it addresses the Five Tools that Gino and I spelled out in *Rocket Fuel*:

1. The Accountability Chart®
2. The Core Questions

3. Rocks
4. The Meeting Pulse®
5. Scorecard

The Accountability Chart

The Accountability Chart is a supercharged organizational chart that goes beyond just showing who reports to whom. It's a tool designed to clarify the structure of your organization, define roles and responsibilities, and ensure accountability flows clearly and effectively. Unlike a traditional org chart, which often focuses on hierarchy, the Accountability Chart is all about function: what needs to get done, who's responsible for doing it, and the one person they're accountable to for that role.

The process starts by asking, "What is the right structure to help us climb this next hill over the next 12–18 months?" You map out the major functions of the business—like Sales & Marketing, Operations, and Finance—and then break those down into specific roles. Each function is a "seat" on the chart, and every seat has clear accountabilities attached to it. The goal is to ensure every function is covered, with no gaps or overlaps, and that the right people are in the right seats. Everyone fits our core values, and has what it takes to perform at the level we need in their seat.

The Accountability Chart is dynamic, and it evolves as your business grows and changes. It's not just a document to file away; it's a living tool that helps you diagnose issues, align your team, and create clarity. When done right, it eliminates confusion, prevents tasks from falling through the cracks, and ensures everyone clearly knows their responsibilities. It's a cornerstone of the EOS Process® and a game-changer for scaling businesses effectively.

The Core Questions

The Core Questions are a set of five critical questions that a Visionary and Integrator must align on to ensure the entire leadership team and organization are all 100 percent on the same page. These questions are foundational to creating clarity and alignment within the business. They include:

What are your core values? These values define the DNA of the people in your organization. Imagine a people magnet: attracting people who fit, and repelling those who don't. They are a filter on the door of your bus that someone must successfully pass through if they're going to get on and ride with us. Once we're on the bus together, these values are our promise to one another for how we're going to show up each day. They define how we're going to play together.

What is your core focus? This is your sweet spot, the intersection of what you're passionate about and what you do best. This is the dent you want to make in the universe, supported by the area you've identified, which gives you the best chance to make that dent. It's also a place where you have a shot to be one of the very best.

What is your core target? An ambitious target on the far horizon (think ten years or so) that provides direction and inspiration. This simple horizon mechanism, when done well, will pass three tests.

- First, it's attractive and motivating. You're drawn toward it, and driven to do whatever it takes to get us there.
- Second, it's aligning. Instead of your team's energy being scattered in multiple directions, we're all focused toward that single point on the horizon. There is tremendous power in having all that human energy focused in a single direction.
- And third, it challenges us to think differently about how we're doing things here today.

We look at the target and smile, because we want it. At the same time, when we look at how we're currently approaching things, we shake our heads. Because our current approach will never get us to that target. This creative tension causes us to stretch our thinking in the present. We begin to think about, talk about, and explore those things that will need to change if we're going to get on a trajectory that will actually move us toward our core target.

What is your marketing strategy? Do you have a clear plan for how you'll attract and retain your ideal customers? This includes a definition of your target market prospects. These are the ones you want to pursue because you think they have the highest probability of converting into your ideal customers. As such, you're willing to invest time, money, and energy in going after them. We can't go after everybody; sales and marketing resources are always limited. So this is how we focus those scarce resources on the group that we expect to give us the greatest overall return. Along with the target market, we must also define our core marketing message. This uniquely answers the question: Why do they choose us over their other alternatives? It's often some variation of better, faster, cheaper, or easier that we're uniquely positioned to deliver. Once we are internally clear on that answer, it becomes much easier to create external marketing and sales messaging that consistently hammers home on those few points. And the promise that we can bring these things together better than anyone else they'll consider.

What is your Three-Year Picture? Envision where you want to be in three years, including key metrics and milestones. This is simply a mid-range snapshot in the direction of your core target. Since it's closer to the present, we can see it in more detail with more granularity. We paint a picture of a future that, if it were true three years from now, would register as a "hell, yeah!" for the entire team. It should always pass those same three tests we outlined for the core target: attractive/motivating, aligning, and challenging.

When these questions are answered and agreed upon, they act as a compass, keeping everyone aligned and moving in the same direction.

Rocks

Rocks are the top three to seven (hopefully much closer to three) priorities your organization or team must accomplish in the next ninety days to stay on track toward your long-term vision. They're called "Rocks" because they represent the big, important tasks that need to be tackled first—before the more minor, less critical stuff fills up your time. The term comes from

Stephen Covey's time-management analogy, where you fit rocks, gravel, sand, and water into a jar. And if you don't put the big rocks in first, they'll never fit.

The process of setting Rocks involves your leadership team coming together every quarter to identify and agree on the most impactful areas of focus to set as your priorities. A good Rock answers the operative question, "What needs to be true (in a given area of focus) for us to feel really good about our progress, that we're highly confident we can achieve by the end of the quarter?" Each Rock is clear. There's no ambiguity. And it will be easy for us to tell (at the end of the quarter) whether it was completed or not. Each Rock is assigned to one owner for accountability. By focusing on Rocks, you create clarity, alignment, and momentum. Breaking your long-term goals into manageable, actionable chunks.

The Meeting Pulse

The Meeting Pulse is the heartbeat of your organization—it's a cadence of regular, structured meetings designed to keep your team aligned, focused, and accountable. It serves as the glue that holds everything together, ensuring that your vision translates into real, measurable traction.

There are three main types of meetings in the Meeting Pulse:

- Annual Meetings: Annual meetings reset your vision, build team health, and create a clear plan for the year ahead. These meetings are held off-site over two days to eliminate distractions and allow the team to focus entirely on working "on" the business, not "in" it. Day one focuses on reviewing the previous year's accomplishments, team health-building exercises, a SWOT analysis, and revisiting your Vision. Day 2 is all about planning. Setting the new one-year plan, establishing Rocks for the first ninety days, and solving key issues that weren't specifically addressed by the plan. This structured approach ensures alignment, clarity, and momentum for the entire organization.

- Quarterly Meetings: These are full-day sessions where your leadership team steps back to review progress, solve big issues, and set Rocks (your top priorities) for the next ninety days. It's a chance to recalibrate and make sure everyone is aligned on the vision and the plan.
- Weekly Meetings: The Level 10 Meeting is a ninety-minute meeting held every week with your leadership team. The agenda is laser-focused on keeping your Rocks on track, solving issues, and maintaining accountability. The name "Level 10" comes from the goal of making these meetings so effective that your team would rate them a 10 out of 10.

The magic of the Meeting Pulse lies in its consistency. By meeting regularly and following a structured agenda, you create a cadence that keeps everyone in sync and ensures that issues are identified and resolved quickly. It's not about having more meetings, it's about having the right meetings. Ones that are productive, focused, and drive results.

Scorecard

A Scorecard is a simple yet powerful tool that gives you a clear, at-a-glance pulse on your business. It's a weekly snapshot of the most critical numbers that tell you how your business is performing and whether you're on track to hit your goals. Think of it as your radar. It helps you spot issues early, predict future outcomes, and make proactive adjustments before problems escalate.

Here's how it works: the Scorecard focuses on a handful of activity-based numbers—typically 5 to 15— that represent the key drivers of your business. These aren't just financial metrics; they're leading indicators from across all areas of the business, like sales, marketing, operations, and customer satisfaction. Each number has a weekly goal, and one person is accountable for driving each measurable. This accountability ensures that nothing falls through the cracks.

The beauty of the Scorecard is its simplicity and focus. It's not overloaded with data. It's streamlined to highlight only the most important metrics. By reviewing it every week in your weekly meetings, you can quickly identify patterns, trends, and issues. If a number isn't hitting its goal, it gets dropped down as an issue to solve during the meeting. Over time, the Scorecard evolves into a tool you love. One that helps you run your business with clarity and confidence.

EOS

While I can't speak for every business OS on the market relative to those Five Tools, I do have direct experience with one proven system that consistently delivers them:

the Entrepreneurial Operating System, or EOS. To learn more, I highly recommend the book *Traction* by Gino Wickman.

EOS is a complete system with simple tools to help you achieve three things we call "Vision, Traction, and Healthy."

- Vision means first getting your leaders 100 percent on the same page with where your organization is going and how it will get there.
- Traction is helping your leaders become more disciplined and accountable, executing at high levels to achieve every part of your Vision.
- Healthy is helping your leaders to become a healthy, functional, cohesive leadership team. Unfortunately, leaders often don't function well as a team.

From there, as goes your leadership team, so goes the rest of your organization. You need to get to the point where your entire organization is crystal clear on your Vision, all much more disciplined and accountable in executing your Vision, gaining consistent Traction, and advancing as a Healthy, functional, cohesive team.

The Six Key Components® of the EOS Model® (Vision, People, Data, Issues, Process, Traction) all work together, and when you're 80 percent strong—or greater—in all of those, that's when you'll truly experience Vision, Traction, and Healthy in your organization.

I touched on this earlier, and some of you may have also heard of something called the EOS Creed: You cannot build a great business on multiple operating systems.

You must choose one. It's more important to have *one* operating system than it is *which one* you choose.

Many companies attempt to take bits and pieces from different systems and cobble them all together. In the end, the system never works well. It creates tons of complexity in the organization. Multiple languages. And it confuses your people.

So please choose one operating system for your business, even if it's other than EOS, and truly commit to mastery.

Now you've seen all four specific types of OS. The sequence begins with your individual perspective, and each added rung brings more depth, ultimately capturing your overall perspective on the business. To climb the OS Ladder[IP], you'll need to have something in place for each rung. To recap, with an example of each:

1. **Individual OS:** The 9 Domains of Freedom (Get your BONUS Mini-Book on *Exponential Freedom via the Resource Page*)

2. **Visionary OS:** The 10 Pillars (the focus of this book)

3. **V/I Duo OS:** The 5 Rules (a focus of *Rocket Fuel*)

4. **Business OS:** EOS (the focus of *Traction*)

Transformation

On the Commit To Your Operating System exercise worksheet below, you'll notice that you have the four different operating systems at the top part of the page, and then the Five Rules and the Five Tools below.

YOUR OS LADDER

OS CATEGORY	SYSTEM	COMMITMENT RATING (1–10)
INDIVIDUAL OS	THE 9 DOMAINS	
VISIONARY OS	THE 10 PILLARS	
V/I DUO OS	THE 5 RULES	
BUSINESS OS	THE 5 TOOLS	

As you rate yourself on each operating system, I want you to ponder just how strong your commitment is to each one. I'm less concerned about how you're currently performing—and more with your level of *commitment*. Are you truly committed to do what is necessary to get this system in place? Think about each and rate yourself.

THE FIVE RULES

RULE	FOCUS	PERFORMANCE RATING (1–10)
1	STAY ON THE SAME PAGE	
2	NO END RUNS	
3	INTEGRATOR IS THE TIE-BREAKER	
4	YOU ARE AN EMPLOYEE WHEN WORKING "IN" THE BUSINESS	
5	MAINTAIN MUTUAL RESPECT	

For the Five Rules, answer how you're doing on each of them. For these, think about your current *performance*. Do you feel like you are staying on the same page with your Integrator? Do you feel like you are correcting and preventing end runs? Are you letting the Integrator be the tiebreaker—and so on down the list?

THE FIVE TOOLS

TOOL	FOCUS	PERFORMANCE RATING (1–10)
1	THE ACCOUNTABILITY CHART	
2	CORE QUESTIONS	
3	ROCKS	
4	THE MEETING PULSE	
5	SCORECARD	

For the Five Tools, answer how you're doing on each of them. For these, think about your current *performance*. Do you feel like your Accountability Chart is clear and up to date? Do you love your answers to the Core Questions? Are you setting and completing great Rocks every ninety days—and so on down the list?

Take five minutes and complete this exercise, making sure to highlight any areas you'd like to discuss further in the Community.

Pillar 4: Commit to Your Operating System

- ☐ Committed to an Individual OS (e.g., 9 Domains of Freedom) to manage their energy, time, and focus.
- ☐ Uses the Visionary OS (10 Pillars) to guide decisions and behavior in their Visionary role.
- ☐ Employs a V/I Duo OS (5 Rules). Partnered with an Integrator and striving to maximize the power of their V/I Duo.
- ☐ Leads within a defined Business OS (e.g., EOS) and is a role model of commitment to that system.

To round out this pillar, review your Visionary Report Card (VRC) above, and read the mindsets that go along with Pillar Four. Give yourself Xs or slashes next to the mindsets you're doing well in, leaving blank the mindsets where you have substantial work to do. Then give yourself a rating on how well you are doing. The scale is 1–10, with 10 being the highest.

Up next, Pillar 5: Support Your Integrator.

PILLAR 5

SUPPORT YOUR INTEGRATOR

The strength of the team is each individual member.
The strength of each member is the team.

—*Phil Jackson*

Support is a simple word. Have you thought much about what it really means? What does it mean to support someone?

It begins with genuinely wanting someone to succeed. You want them to win. In this case, your Integrator. There can't be any part of you that's thinking: "I don't really want this... I don't think it can work... I'm just doing this expecting it to fail... That will show people just how irreplaceable I really am."

If that's where your head is from the jump, the odds are stacked against the relationship. Instead, you must actually see the promise of what a healthy and powerful V/I Duo relationship can do for you and your business.

You want your Integrator to take you another step closer to making that future a reality. As you might expect, this desire is much easier when you are both truly 100 percent on the same page about where you're headed and how you plan to get there. If they win, you win.

Support means you truly care. About them as a human. They're not just a throw-away for you. You chose them carefully. And you care enough to truly invest in them, as a person, and build a meaningful relationship with them. You also want them to grow individually through this experience. And someday, even if this business outgrows them, or they outgrow this business, you'll take pride in seeing them rewarded for the time they've spent with you.

Because you actually want them to win, you're also willing to be there when they need you. You show up for them. Sometimes this is demonstrated by being accessible. Or it might be through consistent communication. Or maybe you back them up when things get crazy, which they will. And when that happens, you must come alongside them and navigate the chaos together.

Picture the two of you in a canoe. Always together. At times, you're floating calmly, individually attending to whatever is needed. You know they're right there if you need them. Then you have your regular aligning communication, checking the map for the next stop along the route. And then you hit the rapids. Focus heightens. One hundred percent aligned, you two execute harmoniously to navigate the stretch of chaos. Rapidly adjusting to each new obstacle or opportunity that presents itself. You safely exit the other end and celebrate your accomplishment. What did we learn from that run that will make us even better in the next one? Anchor that learning by talking it out, and the journey continues.

Support means you encourage them—honestly. This involves so much more than just "blowing sunshine" at them. Help them see why you believe they can do it. Don't ignore the challenges you may see for them along the way. Share the evidence you see. Remind them about the times you've already seen them do something just like this. And, if you see an area where they still need to grow—or even fix an approach that hasn't been working well for them—point that out as well. Give them concrete examples of whatever you've observed that put it on your radar. Maybe you've noticed that every time they work on an issue that would benefit from getting more people bought in up front, they tend to get overly anxious and move ahead too fast. This mucks things up later, when they have to go back and repair the damage. Help them see this pattern, and offer advice about how to generate more support earlier in the process.

I love the old Clint Eastwood film *The Good, the Bad, and the Ugly*. When you think about healthy "support," your journey will certainly include all three. It will most assuredly be dynamic. Count on it. Change is the only constant.

Finally, don't make the job harder for your Integrator than it already is. The hill is steep enough without you stirring up messes that they must repeatedly circle back to clean up. Don't make them hound you just to get on the same page. And don't sow seeds of doubt with others in the organization. If you're not confident in them, what chance do they have to earn the confidence of the rest of the team?

Disclaimer: If your Integrator always seems to find a way to make you crazy through their decisions and choices, that may not be the right Integrator for you. This does happen. If so, you'll need to fire them and try again. Hopefully, you'll be smarter from the experience.

Knowing When It's Not Just "Healthy Tension"

Some tension is normal and necessary in a strong V/I Duo. You're wired differently. That friction creates the spark. It fuels better decisions, more complete perspectives, and a stronger organization.

But there's a line. How do you know when it's crossed?

Watch for these warning signs:

- **Trust is gone.** You're second-guessing every decision. You're walking on eggshells.
- **You've stopped having honest conversations.** One of you is holding back, or you're stuck in a loop of constant conflict. Communication has broken down.
- **You're doing their job (again).** You've taken back things you were supposed to let go of. Or they've checked out.
- **Progress has stopped.** You're no longer learning or improving. You've had the same arguments for months. Nothing's changing.
- **There's a pattern of disrespect.** Undermining, public or private, is never okay. One negative comment can trigger a cultural cancer.

> If this sounds familiar, lean in harder. Try to repair the relationship. Return to the 5 Rules. Double down on Same Page Meetings. Get outside help.
>
> However, if you've done the work and the issues persist. It may be time to move on.
>
> You're not giving up. You're smarter from the experience and making room for the right fit.

The Commitments

Supporting your Integrator requires your commitment. In particular, you will need to make four essential commitments to master this Pillar.

You commit to climbing the OS Ladder. That means you commit to each of the operating systems in Pillar 4. That doesn't mean you're all the way there right now, but you will climb and strive to master each one.

You commit to publicly supporting your Integrator. Nobody can do more to help them be successful than you can. You must inspire confidence. If you believe in them, they'll believe in them! If you help them get some early wins, everybody is going to believe more and have more confidence. Help them develop winning plans. Not only the long-term plan, but the short-term plans as well. Help them get some early wins.

You commit to do the work. It's a relationship, and like all relationships, it takes work. Some of my clients call them their "business spouse." Think of how much work that relationship requires and deserves!

You commit to check your ego. A lot of people violate this one, so I need you to be aware. Play at eye-level with your Integrator. If you don't feel you can play at eye level, you may not have the right Integrator. You're strong; you need an Integrator who's just as strong. You don't want to be able to mow over them every time you have a new idea of something you want to do. Balance in power and mutual respect are essential. Neither will ever make a negative comment about the other to anyone else.

You must commit to each of these and support your Integrator 100 percent.

In addition, you commit to regularly (at least quarterly) using the three specific tools we've created to help you maximize this vital V/I Duo relationship:

- Rocket Fuel Power Index
- Integrator Report Card
- Visionary Report Card (which you've already begun)

Rocket Fuel Power Index

As Gino and I began teaching the Five Rules, we saw that it would be helpful for each V/I Duo to have a tool that could show them how well they were doing—how much power their Duo was currently generating. This also happened at a time when Dan Sullivan was teaching us about Mindset Scorecards. We wanted a simple scorecard framework to help you get more of the great relationships you really want while avoiding more of the bad ones you don't. You identify the key selection/

avoidance criteria, and then build out a descriptive range from worst case to best case for each.

Combining the two, our next tool—the Rocket Fuel Power Index—came together while Gino and I sat together during one of our Strategic Coach workshops with Dan in Chicago. Since then, thousands of Visionaries and Integrators have used it to help them see where they can improve their V/I relationship.

ROCKET FUEL POWER INDEX

Maximize Your Visionary + Integrator Relationship

MINDSETS		2	3	4	5	6	7	8	9	10	NOW	NEXT
1. Vision Alignment												
2. Staying in Sync												
3. Commitment to Same Page Meeting*												
4. Open/Honest Communication												
5. Mutual Respect												
6. Role Clarity												
7. Agreement on 90-Day Priorities												
8. Engagement with Leadership Team												
										YOUR SCORE		

The Rocket Fuel Power Index focuses on eight vital mindsets related to the V/I Duo relationship.

VisionaryBook.com

Think about the current state of your Visionary/ Integrator relationship. I'll walk you through each of the eight mindsets, showing you what each end of the scale looks like. You also have a couple of options that fall in between. Each of the different columns reflects different degrees of health, if you will, in each of the mindset areas. As I present each one, I want you to imagine where you fall on that spectrum. I suggest you do this in two steps. First, decide which of the four major ranges feels right. Then, decide where you fall within that range. Pick a number along the spectrum for each mindset, and write it in the "Now" column for that row. This is a moment in time snapshot, so please don't overweigh the past nor your hopes for the future. Capture how you feel today.

Vision Alignment

On the low end, we don't agree on how fast we want to grow our plans and ideas for the future. We want to do what we want to do.

On the high end, we completely agree on who we are as a company, what we do, why we do it, and where we are going.

MINDSETS	1 2 3	4 5 6	7 8 9	10 11 12
1. Vision Alignment	We don't agree on how fast we want to grow, or our plans and ideas for the future. We just want to do what we want to do.	We are often at odds about the vision for the future of the company.	Most of the time we agree on the vision, although there are a few disconnects.	We completely agree on who we are as a company, what we do, why we do it, and where we are going.

A ship cannot travel to two different ports simultaneously. Ultimately, we want everyone in the organization—all of the energy arrows—pointed in the same direction. It all starts with the V/I Duo being completely aligned.

Staying in Sync

On the low end, we never seem to agree on any issues. It's like we're speaking two languages.

On the high end, we are 100 percent in sync. We resolve issues between us quickly. While we disagree on some issues, we always resolve them.

MINDSETS	1 2 3	4 5 6	7 8 9	10 11 12
2. Staying in Sync	We never seem to agree on any issues. It's like we are speaking two different languages.	Of all the issues we are facing as a company, we seem to agree on about half. The other half we avoid.	We have a high level of "same pageness," although there are some issues that we still avoid.	We are 100% in sync. We resolve issues between us quickly. While we disagree on some things, we always resolve it.

Trust in each other. You are two halves of the same brain, speaking the same language. While your minds are very different, there is enough convergence to make your Duo effective.

Commitment to the Same Page Meeting

On the low end, we never hold Same Page Meetings. We don't think they're necessary.

On the high end, we meet every month and resolve every issue. We feel they are vital to our success.

MINDSETS	1 2 3	4 5 6	7 8 9	10 11 12
3. Commitment to Same Page Meeting*	We never do our Same Page Meetings. We don't think they are necessary.	We schedule our Same Page Meetings but cancel or reschedule them most of the time.	We commit to (and hold) most of our Same Page Meetings. They are relatively productive.	We meet every month for a Same Page Meeting and resolve every issue. We feel they are vital to our success.

We made this the number 1 Rule of the 5 Rules for a reason. It is absolutely vital and so easy to take for granted. It may be simple, just not always easy. Like most things in life.

Open and Honest Communication

On the low end, we both hold back. We never share issues we are having, or how we are truly feeling.

On the high end, we openly and quickly share any issues that we have with each other, and we always know exactly how the other is feeling.

MINDSETS	1 2 3	4 5 6	7 8 9	10 11 12
4. Open/Honest Communication	We both hold back. We never share issues we are having or how we are truly feeling.	We share issues with each other but in a passive-aggressive way, and usually not until things come to a head.	We are open and honest about issues but get uncomfortable having conflict. We lack comfort in sharing our feelings.	We openly and quickly share any issues that we have with each other, and always know exactly how the other is feeling.

Get the important issues out on the table. If you keep anything inside, you have no chance to work on it. Don't expect your counterpart to be a mindreader. You owe it to them to let them know. As you're laying out the problem, don't spin it. Strive for raw, unvarnished truth. "This is how I really see it, how I really feel about it." Simply let it fly. That will give you both the best chance of being able to work together and solve it.

Mutual Respect

On the low end, we make negative comments about each other to others in the company. We don't value each other's contributions.

On the high end, we never make a negative comment about the other. We both feel the other has our back. We have mutual respect. End runs do not happen.

	MINDSETS	1	2	3	4	5	6	7	8	9	10		
5.	Mutual Respect	We make negative comments about each other to others in the company. We don't value each other's contributions.			We don't make negative comments, but we still have the occasional eye roll. We lack trust and do "end runs."			We respect each other but still do the occasional "end run."			We never make a negative comment about the other. We both feel the other has our back. We have mutual respect. "End runs" don't happen.		

Life is too short to work with someone you don't respect, or that doesn't respect you. In addition, this relationship is too important to let it be anything less. Work diligently to build and maintain this mutual respect. If not, don't be surprised if you find yourself sitting at the helm alone.

Role Clarity

On the low end, we're constantly tripping over each other, duplicating efforts, and questioning what the other does.

On the high end, we completely understand each other's roles and believe the other brings tremendous value. Our puzzle pieces fit

MINDSETS	1 2 3	4 5 6	7 8	9
6. Role Clarity	We are constantly tripping over each other, duplicating efforts and questioning what the other does.	Roles are relatively clear. We still have overlap. Employees are still confused about what a Visionary and Integrator do.	The Integrator is 80% the tiebreaker and runs the day-to-day. The Visionary is 80% the idea person and vision holder.	We completely understand each other's roles and believe the other brings tremendous value. Our "puzzle pieces" fit.

Role clarity means assigning who does what from the start and then living by it! When you see an unclear role, don't let it slide. These are the crossed wires that keep interfering.

Agreement on the 90-Day Priorities

On the low end, three-month priorities are not established. We never agree on what's important. We have multiple competing priorities.

On the high end, we're in lockstep on what the three to seven most important priorities are for the next ninety days. We execute them well.

MINDSETS	1 2 3	4 5 6	7 8	9
7. Agreement on 90-Day Priorities	Short-term priorities are not established. We never agree on what's important now. We have multiple competing priorities.	We set 90-day priorities, but they constantly change during the quarter. It's like a moving target.	We know our 90-day priorities and do a pretty good job staying focused on them.	We are in lockstep on what the 3-7 most important priorities are for the next 90 days. We execute them well.

Ninety days is just the right length for our human brains. Long enough to make significant progress, yet short enough for us to not lose sight of why we chose it as our focus.

Let's say you and your Integrator are prepping for the next quarter. You're both seeing some big opportunities plus a few fires to put out. You suggest launching a new marketing initiative to drive leads. Your Integrator brings up a major system upgrade that's been causing pain for months. Instead of locking horns, you step back together and ask: "What really matters most right now? Which has the highest magnitude of impact?"

After some healthy debate, you align around three clear priorities:

1. Fix the system upgrade issue to stabilize operations.
2. Roll out the new lead-gen campaign, *but only* after the ops fix is underway.
3. Level up the leadership team's accountability by refining departmental scorecards.

Now you're aligned. You know the *why* behind each priority. And for the next ninety days, every decision, meeting, and resource allocation is filtered through that lens. That's the power of a locked-in Duo.

Engagement with the Leadership Team

On the low end, we don't have weekly meetings with our leadership team.

On the high end, we attend every leadership team meeting and are fully engaged. Meetings are lively and interesting, never boring.

	MINDSETS	1 2 3	4 5 6	7	8 9 10
8.	Engagement with Leadership Team	We don't have weekly meetings with our leadership team.	We do have weekly meetings with our leadership team, however, one of us is usually distracted, unengaged, or absent.	We both attend the weekly leadership meeting most of the time, and the meetings are moderately effective.	We attend every leadership team meeting and are fully engaged. Meetings are lively, interesting, and never boring.

As we've discussed, support involves being there. Enough to make it obvious that we're all together in the same boat. When you skip leadership meetings or just phone it in, it sends the message: *This doesn't matter.* You weaken your Integrator's position and leave the team confused or second-guessing.

Absentee Visionaries create a power vacuum. People wonder what's really important, what's changing behind the scenes, and whether they're still on track.

But when you consistently show up—attentive, aligned, engaged—it reinforces clarity and confidence. It shows your Integrator has your full backing, and the whole team is rowing in the same direction. You don't need to steer every moment. Just be in the boat. Eyes up. Present. Focused. That alone can change everything.

Once you've written down your score for each mindset, you should use it in a conversation with your Integrator. Just as you've taken it, your Integrator will take it. Then sit down across the table from each other and walk through it together. This is a great discussion for a Same Page Meeting.

Compare notes with each other. Some things you may be perfectly aligned on. Yet that's not where you want to spend most of your time talking. You want to dig into where you're in disagreement. And try to understand why you're seeing the topic so differently. Communication is missing there. You want to see the same issues and interpret them in the same way.

"On this item, I said we're a nine. What'd you say? You said we're a four. Okay, that's quite a bit different. Help me understand how you see it that way. Why not higher, why not lower?"

Wherever you see a difference, discuss it. That will help bring you back into alignment. The discussion may bring other problems to the surface. "Wow, I wasn't aware of that. I was thinking about it differently."

Openly talking helps you get realigned and back on the same page.

You should prioritize one or two mindset areas to improve every quarter. Be sure to tally up your total in the "Now" column. That's your baseline. You and your Integrator can begin to chip away at those areas and see your V/I Duo power increase.

Whenever I talk to groups about these mindsets, two of them always tend to score the lowest. And also show the greatest gap between the Visionary and the Integrator. Can you guess what they are? Yep, two of the simplest: Role Clarity and Commitment to the Same Page Meeting! So please make sure you're doing really well on both of those.

Integrator Report Card

As you support your Integrator, another powerful tool is called the Integrator Report Card. It's similar to the Visionary Report Card, only it's used as a way for you to grade how well your Integrator is doing.

Just as the Visionary Report Card covers the 10 Pillars of becoming a great Visionary, the Integrator Report Card focuses on the areas an Integrator must master to become truly great.

Integrator Report Card

- Check each sub-area where your Integrator is consistently achieving success.
- Rate each major area on a scale of 1-10 (10 being best).

Major Area	Sub-Area		1-10
1. The Five Rules	The Integrator works with the Visionary to ensure that we consistently follow the disciplines of the 5 Rules.	☐	
	V/I are consistently on the same page.	☐	
	V/I show each other mutual respect.	☐	
	V/I have eliminated end runs.	☐	
	The Integrator breaks the ties.	☐	
	Any/all owners behave as model employees when working "in" the business.	☐	
2. The Five Tools (+OS)	The Integrator works with the Visionary to ensure that we consistently follow the disciplines of the 5 Tools.	☐	
	We have selected and implemented an Operating System, and it is adhered to by everyone.	☐	
	V/I are solidly aligned around the Core Questions (V/TO®), and that plan is shared by the organization.	☐	

Major Area	Sub-Area		1-10
	The Accountability Chart® is complete and constantly updated; everyone is clearly accountable for their seat(s).	☐	
	Everyone has meaningful Rocks, and our completion rates are consistently 80 percent or better.	☐	
	Everyone is engaged in a weekly Level 10 Meeting®, where they are reviewing results, solving issues, and staying connected.	☐	
	We have a weekly Scorecard that gives us a pulse on the business and helps us spot issues earlier.	☐	
3. Visionary Relationship	The V/I Connector Scores indicate a strong V/I Duo fit.	☐	
	The Integrator has the skills/ competencies needed for this business. (Integrator Spectrum fit).	☐	
	The Visionary has a high level of trust with the Integrator and spends most time/energy in their area of unique giftedness, or "sweet spot."	☐	
	The Integrator consistently takes the Visionary's ideas and makes them happen.	☐	
	The Integrator effectively harnesses the best ideas and the unique energy of the Visionary.	☐	

Major Area	Sub-Area		1-10
	The Integrator effectively "translates" the Visionary's vision to the team.	☐	
	The Integrator references the Visionary's Wish List to provide planning and priorities.	☐	
	The Integrator effectively compartmentalizes the Visionary's ideas, so the Visionary feels that every idea has a place and is not getting lost.	☐	
	The Rocket Fuel™ Power Index is completed and discussed every 90 days (at least), with steadily improving alignment and scores.	☐	
4. Results	The Integrator executes the business plan and consistently exceeds P&L objectives.	☐	
	The major functions of the business (sales/marketing, operations, finance/admin) ALL work well.	☐	
	The leadership team consistently chooses the right priorities and delivers on them.	☐	
	The Integrator keeps things on track NOW... the trains consistently run on time.	☐	
5. Team Alignment	There is clearly "One Team."	☐	
	The Integrator harmoniously integrates the major functions.	☐	

Major Area	Sub-Area		1-10
	Cross-functional issues are effectively identified and resolved.	☐	
	V/I + leadership team are consistently aligned with one another and the rest of the organization.	☐	
	Communication flows freely across the organization.	☐	
	Messages cascade effectively, so there are no surprises.	☐	
6. Team Health	The leadership team is a model of "Team Health" for the organization.	☐	
	We have a strong foundation of vulnerability-based trust.	☐	
	Conflict is healthy and comes from a place of seeking to understand different perspectives.	☐	
	Commitments are meaningful—we do what we say we will.	☐	
	Accountability is expected and embraced.	☐	
	We are consistently focused on the specific results we want to achieve and not afraid to discuss them.	☐	
7. People	Every person in the organization is a Right Person (fits our Core Values).	☐	
	Every person is a Right Seat (GWCs their seat in The Accountability Chart).	☐	

Major Area	Sub-Area		1-10
8. Leadership, Management, and Accountability	The Integrator is a role model for effective Leadership and Management.	☐	
	The Integrator is continually developing those abilities in their direct reports.	☐	
	Accountability is strong across the leadership team.	☐	
	Everyone in the organization with direct reports is delivering effective Leadership and Management to each of them.	☐	
	Accountability is strong across the organization.	☐	
	The Integrator demonstrates high emotional intelligence (EQ) when dealing with people.	☐	
	The Integrator is emotionally stable and confident, which inspires confidence in others.	☐	
9. Core Processes	Our 6-10 Core Processes are documented.	☐	
	Our 6-10 Core Processes are simplified.	☐	
	Our 6-10 Core Processes are Followed by All (train, measure, manage, update).	☐	
	We have a "Company Way" document that pulls our Core Processes together.	☐	
	We experience improved scalability and consistency.	☐	

Major Area	Sub-Area		1-10
10. Continual Improvement	The Integrator is continually looking for ways to improve capacity, speed, and quality.	☐	
	The Integrator is obsessed with simplification.	☐	
	The Integrator creates capacity via delegation, systems, and processes.	☐	
	Problems and obstacles are quickly identified and articulated.	☐	
	The Integrator leverages analysis and deductive reasoning to create and implement effective solutions.	☐	
	All leaders are expected to make decisions, build capacity, and find ways to get stuff done through others.	☐	
Total Score:			

You'll follow the same procedure you did with the Rocket Fuel Power Index. The Visionary and Integrator will each fill out their own Integrator Report Card. Then you'll sit down together in your Same Page Meeting and compare the results. Acknowledge what you're seeing the same way and explore what you're seeing differently. Do this at least once per quarter. I'd suggest doing this exercise monthly until you are closely aligned. Then you can back off to discussing it quarterly.

This will help your Integrator get crystal clear on how they're doing relative to your expectations.

We use both the Rocket Fuel Power Index and the Integrator Report Card as accountability tools for the members of the Integrator Mastery Forum™.

The Integrator Mastery Forum (IMF) brings together like-minded Integrators who are all-in on growth, mastery, and leading alongside their Visionary in a strong V/I Duo. It's a peer group experience designed specifically for Integrators who want to sharpen their skills, solve real issues, and increase the power of their Duo. Members meet regularly, share tools like the Rocket Fuel Power Index and Integrator Report Card, and support each other in becoming truly great at the Integrator role.

When the member Integrators come together in a Quarterly Integrator Exchange® (QIE®), they will bring these two tools to review for accountability. And they may even work on specific issues to help them improve on both. How can they get even better individually as an Integrator? And how can they increase the power of their V/I Duo relationship? We spoke earlier about the power of a peer group. And this has proven to be a valuable resource for the Integrators involved. My Integrator is a member, and we faithfully prepare our Rocket Fuel Power Index and the Integrator Report Card each quarter. We always notice something we can improve.

One Visionary I worked with—let's call her Susan—made this a consistent practice. Each quarter, she and her Integrator filled out their Rocket Fuel Power Index and Integrator Report Card separately, then compared notes in their Same Page Meeting. At first, the conversations were a little awkward. But by the third quarter, they were unlocking real breakthroughs. They realized they'd missed two important areas: (1) hard conversations about long-term vision, which led to months of crossed wires, and (2) highlighting the work the Integrator still needed to do on Core Processes. Now the Same Page Meeting is one of their most trusted rituals. Susan told me, "It's like recalibrating the compass every ninety days. We never drift too far off course." Two years in, this Duo had increased their Power Index score by over twenty-five points!

Transformation

Rocket Fuel Power Index

Download the Rocket Fuel Power Index. Score yourself in each of the eight mindset areas. Then ask your Integrator to do the same on their own copy. Bring both versions to your next Same Page Meeting and walk through them together.

VisionaryBook.com

Total RFPI Score: _____
Where are you most aligned? What do you feel good about?
Where are the biggest gaps? What are you concerned about?
Which one or two mindset areas will you focus on improving over the next ninety days?

Integrator Report Card

Download the Integrator Report Card. Complete your evaluation of how well your Integrator is performing in each area. Have your Integrator complete their own version as well. Bring both to your Same Page Meeting and discuss.

VisionaryBook.com

Total IRC Score: _____

Where are they strongest? What do you feel good about? Where do you see room for growth? What are you concerned about?

Choose one area to focus on improving over the next ninety days.

Visionary Commitments Self-Check

For each of the five commitments below, rate your commitment level (1-10):

I COMMIT TO...	COMMITMENT RATING (1–10)
Climbing the OS Ladder. (Pillar 4)	
Publicly supporting my Integrator.	
Doing the work of building a great V/I relationship.	
Checking my ego and playing at eye level.	
Using the V/I tools every quarter: Rocket Fuel Power Index, Integrator Report Card, and Visionary Report Card.	

Where are you doing well?
Which areas still need attention?
Make sure to highlight any areas you'd like to discuss in the Community.

VisionaryBook.com

Pillar 5: Support Your Integrator

- ☐ Climbing the OS Ladder.
- ☐ Consistently shows public support for their Integrator.
- ☐ Wants the Integrator to win and is doing their part to make that outcome real.
- ☐ Fully committed to the Same Page Meeting uses it to strengthen clarity, resolve tension, and reinforce alignment.
- ☐ Challenges the Integrator in healthy ways, but avoids patterns of sabotage, tampering, or withholding.
- ☐ Using the V/I Tools (RFPI, IRC, VRC) completed and discussed every ninety days (at least), with steadily improving alignment and scores.

To round out this pillar, review your Visionary Report Card (VRC) and read the mindsets above that go along with Pillar 5. Give yourself Xs or slashes next to the mindsets you're doing well in, leaving blank the mindsets where you have substantial work to do. Then give yourself a rating on how well you are doing. The scale is 1–10, with 10 being the highest.

Up next, Pillar 6: Think About What You Think About.

PILLAR 6

THINK ABOUT WHAT YOU THINK ABOUT

Our life is what our thoughts make it.

—*Marcus Aurelius*

Now that you've grounded your external systems and relationships, it's time to turn inward, where the real battle often takes place.

Can you recall a time in your life when someone you knew was dealt a really bad hand? Yet somehow, against all odds, they kept a positive outlook?

I once had a business partner who lost his wife. Let's call him Scott. The two had been extremely close, doing everything together. Her battle with cancer was a long, drawn-out, agonizing journey. Scott lost a little more of her each day. And then she was gone. The grief was incredibly difficult for Scott to process. He would break down often. He needed help. Thankfully, he started seeing a professional to help him work through it.

Scott got better. He began to function again. One day, I asked him, "Scott, what helped you recover the most?" His response stuck with me: "They taught me to think about what I think about. It's the one thing I can control. I've realized that some thoughts just take me down a very dark path—to no good end. Now whenever I notice that happening, I interrupt the pattern and replace it with a thought that is helpful for me."

It worked for Scott. And it can work for you.

You can manage your thinking. That space between your ears. You can either focus on the negative and fall into a dark hole or shift your mindset to focus on the positive things around you.

If you consider what Visionaries tend to think about, you realize that some of the agonizing is simply not helpful for you. In particular, I've found seven different mindsets you must actively manage. Let's go through those now.

Patience

Being patient may be the most difficult ask I can make of you.

It turns out that being patient is not easy for most Visionaries. It isn't on your list of superpowers. You're likely not naturally wired for it. In fact, you're probably wired for exactly the opposite.

As a result, when you bring in an Integrator, you'll want them to accomplish everything, all the time, right now. And it's not going to happen that way. You need to be aware of that going in. Use the tools to clarify what's most important. And it can't be everything. "If everything's important, nothing is important."

Focus on your wish list. Focus on your vision. Focus on getting aligned around priorities.

Set a plan. More than likely, you two will need at least a year to hit your stride as a V/I Duo. So plan how you're going to rack up some early wins in the first one hundred days. A good beginning is very important. In fact, there's a great book called *The First 90 Days* by Michael D. Watkins that can help you even more with this. Hand your new Integrator a simple plan that shows them what good work looks like from day one. Help them grab quick wins—like fixing an easy problem or making one small process better. Those early victories build confidence and earn trust from the entire team. Learn fast. Talk with key people often. And follow the plan together. Through it all, be patient.

Become two halves of the same brain. Hold monthly Same Page Meetings; maybe even hold them more frequently in those early days. Discuss the Rocket Fuel Power Index. Talk through the Integrator Report Card. And be patient.

Work the EOS process. Maintain a healthy meeting pulse. You'll both engage fully with the rest of your leadership team in ninety-minute weekly meetings, one-day quarterlies, and two-day annuals. Bring it all back together with a quarterly all-hands, and provide a State of the Company update for everyone. And make sure everyone in the organization is having a Quarterly Conversation with their direct manager—more often if there are issues. This will ensure that expectations are crystal clear and provide consistent accountability for meeting them. And, during all of this, be patient.

Asking you to be patient is like asking a boxer not to fight. It goes against your natural instinct. That said, I do ask you to be patient until it's time to not be patient. While I won't exactly be standing there to tell you when that is, you will have all the tools from this book to help you see that moment.

Out to Pasture

Some Visionaries hit a strange point after elevating out of the weeds. They feel "put out to pasture."

Before, you were in everything. You probably built the company that way, out of necessity. But then you hired a strong Integrator, built a leadership team, and handed off most of the doing. Suddenly, your calendar looks different. Your inbox is lighter. And instead of feeling freed, you start wondering, *Do they even need me anymore?*

The truth? You're needed more than ever, just in a different way. Not to jump back into the weeds, but to spend time in that Visionary headspace where you see the future, spot opportunity, and connect the dots others can't. That's your Intrinsic Genius. It's high-value work only you can do.

Melissa, founder of a fast-growing marketing tech company, hit this wall hard. In the early years, she did everything. After hiring a strong Integrator, she felt useless: "Like they don't need me anymore."

We dug in. I asked, "When you're not forcing yourself into the day-to-day, where does your mind go?"

She paused. "Big stuff. Industry changes. Partnerships. Things that could double us again in two years. But that stuff doesn't feel like work."

That was the breakthrough. Visionary work may not feel like work to you. But it's the most valuable contribution you can make.

Melissa carved out weekly "Blue Sky" time to think and explore, then vetted ideas with her Integrator in Same Page Meetings. The business grew faster, and she felt more energized than ever. Her advice now looks different:

"Don't fight the feeling. Embrace your headspace. That's where the real breakthroughs live."

> That was the breakthrough. Visionary work may not feel like work to you. But it's the most valuable contribution you can make.

The fix: Reframe the feeling. Stay engaged through your meetings and Scorecard. Protect time for high-value Visionary thinking. And remember, this isn't being "put out to pasture." It's finally being in the driver's seat.

This feeling may come and go in cycles. At first, you might think, *I'm not needed anymore!* Then you'll realize you're working in your sweet spot. And that's when it hits you: *This is exactly where I'm supposed to be.*

Gratitude

Sometimes the only way to shift your mindset is by *changing the lens entirely.*

One of my clients experienced a tragedy no parent should have to face: the loss of a child. Devastating. The grief was total. It overwhelmed everything.

Eventually, when he was able to start talking about it, he shared what helped him endure. His insight was simple and unforgettable: "Gratitude."

He told me that every day, sometimes multiple times a day, he forced himself to find something to be grateful for. Some days, it was big—like the support of his wife, or the strength of his faith. Other days, it was something as small as sunlight through a window. It didn't erase the pain. But it gave him a place to stand. A path forward. A way to keep living.

And he did.

That story never left me. It's a powerful reminder that gratitude is not just a warm, fuzzy feeling. It's a mental discipline. A choice. A daily practice.

As a Visionary, you'll face seasons of chaos, disappointment, and frustration. Ideas that don't land. Hires that don't work. People who let you down. But even then, you can choose your focus.

You can focus on what's broken, or you can focus on what's working.

You can focus on what's missing, or you can focus on what you've put in place.

You can focus on how far you have to go, or you can focus on how far you've already come. Dan Sullivan calls this thinking "The Gap or The Gain."

Gratitude doesn't mean settling. It doesn't mean ignoring problems. But it does mean rooting your mindset in a more productive place. It grounds you. Clears the fog. And gives you the energy to keep moving forward.

A negative thought cannot simultaneously exist in a mind filled with gratitude.

Intellectual Humility

There's another mindset I want to challenge you to adopt. I believe it's shared by every truly great Visionary

I've ever worked with. And I believe it might be the rarest trait of all:

Intellectual humility.

It's the ability to hold your beliefs loosely. To ask questions, instead of making declarations. To be curious when challenged, rather than defensive.

I carry a note card with four questions to remind me of this mindset. I came across it through author Daniel Pink, who got it from Warren Berger. Berger laid out these simple questions to help assess your own intellectual humility:

1. Do I think more like a soldier or a scout?

   Soldiers defend positions. Scouts explore new territory.

2. Would I rather be right or would I rather understand?

3. Do I actively seek out opposing views?

4. Do I enjoy the pleasant surprise of discovering I'm mistaken?

Those questions hit me pretty hard the first time I read them. And they continue to challenge me daily.

Because here's the truth: as a Visionary, your ideas are powerful. But if you become too attached to being *right*, those ideas can calcify. They stop evolving. They stop *working*.

The best Visionaries I know are students—always learning, always adjusting, always scouting the next hill. They stay open. They listen. They're willing to be wrong in pursuit of what's *right*.

Ask yourself those four questions now. See where you stand. And see how shifting your posture might open a few doors that you didn't even realize were closed. And if you're at all like me, you may need a reminder on this one from time to time. Which is why I carry the card!

Trust vs. Control

The "out to pasture" feeling relates to this mindset. Gino and I interviewed a lot of Visionaries when doing research for the *Rocket Fuel* book. I remember coming into those conversations with a presumption that we would find Visionaries struggled with the need to control. It appeared they were controlling by nature, and they needed to hold onto responsibilities to control them.

As we talked to more and more Visionaries, it became apparent that the issue wasn't really control. Visionaries told me, "I'd love to get this off my plate. And not have to worry about it anymore." But they don't. They would say, "I really do want to let it go, but I'm afraid." When we dug into why they were reluctant, we discovered painful experiences in their past.

At some point, there was something special that they'd built or created. They asked someone, "Here you go. Will you take care of this for me?" And they handed off their "baby" and walked away hopeful. Only to watch helplessly as this person then dropped it on the floor. It shattered into a thousand pieces. They were left there, putting all those pieces back together, wondering what had just happened. Was it because they gave up control?

Sometimes they'd decide to trust someone again, and the same thing would happen. They had repeated experiences where they've handed off something important, people dropped the ball, and it cost them.

You too may be scarred by that type of experience. If so, you must work on rebuilding your ability to trust people. Not blindly, but with intent. Know that you can hand off something important—in the right way to the right person—and it can work out well.

How you choose whom to trust depends on how you engage in the relationship to build that trust. Make sure they are the right person for the job. Are they wired for this? Do they want to do it? Are their capabilities at the level necessary to deliver a strong performance? You must set forth crystal-clear expectations, and you must follow up to ensure success. Put measurables in place. Inspect what you expect. All these things are within your control.

Building trust doesn't happen fast; it takes time and intention. And you can work on that too. Remember patience? The right people will work with you to build that foundation of trust.

Being open to building such a foundation is especially important with your Integrator. Share your internal conflict with them. "This is my issue. If you show me you can do this, I'll feel a lot better."

Trust is a journey. It takes time. And it never ends.

Guidance without Tampering

Guidance is a Visionary function; tampering is not. You don't mean to tamper. You don't mean to be disruptive. But old habits die hard. You've been doing so many jobs from the beginning. Because of that, you go talk to somebody and end up telling them what to do. You make the decision. Meanwhile, your Integrator just spent who knows how much time teeing up what to do, setting it up in the context of everything else that's going on. Then you just came along and messed up all of it.

We mentioned end runs earlier. You shouldn't be walking right past your Integrator, going out into the organization, and delivering orders off the cuff. We need you to be a teacher. We need you to be a coach. Take all that you know and begin to institutionalize it in a way that is readily accessible by anyone who needs it whenever they need it. Even when you're not around. Document that mental checklist you instinctively go through when evaluating certain situations. Have someone record you telling those stories that embody the vital elements of your culture. Get that epic client story captured in a way that future generations will be able to see how we all worked together to deliver such an amazing result. Embed your wisdom in the core fabric of the organization.

In order to guide your people, you must talk to your people; exchange information. Listen to them, and tune into what's going on. Then use what you gather to guide, coach, and develop them. Take what you've learned and generate new ideas. Feed all that information back to your Integrator. Then they can go and execute what you want done. Allow them the chance to work your idea through the organization properly, with accountability and follow-through. Progress will happen instead of splintered motion. You'll take comfort in knowing their trusted hand is at the steering wheel along the way.

In one extreme example, a well-meaning Visionary of a fifty-person company simply couldn't control himself. He effectively wandered around the office, meddling in whatever happened to be going on at that moment. People were left scrambling, and the Integrator seemed to continuously circle around and clean up after him. Fortunately, his Integrator was strong enough to confront him about it. She shared evidence from the people impacted and was able to convince him to run an experiment where he worked outside the office for a period of time, away from the temptation to tamper. The positive results were immediate and obvious to all. The distraction factor dropped for everyone, and productivity skyrocketed. Realizing this, the Visionary was able to redirect his energy into being much more of a teacher and a coach, turning his presence in the office once again into a positive influence for everyone.

Divergent Thinking

The final mindset in this Pillar stems from a session I had with one of my private clients. Candidly, it emerged during a burst of my own frustration. It was a familiar pattern, which I had never before seen taken to such an extreme. The thinking patterns of a Visionary and an Integrator are very, very different. A Visionary loves to play in a divergent space, where all the options are available. You don't want to close any off because they could be really good. Especially if you thought of it.

You are wired to think more is better. You want to do all this stuff. You don't want to let any of it get lost. And yet you also know—deep down inside—that the company can't do everything. If we try to do everything, we won't get anywhere.

Luckily for you, the Integrator is wired exactly the opposite. They try to take all of these ideas and distill them into the one thing they'll need to focus on executing. If you bring a pile of new ideas to a meeting, they're likely to say, "Let's take this one off." And you think, "I don't want to take that one off, it's a good one! I want to keep all of these."

Your divergent thinking plus their convergent thinking forms a pattern. It repeats over and over again. The Visionary starts to run rampant with their ideas, while the Integrator is trying to narrow them back down.

Divergent: expanding all the possibilities. This is how *you* are wired.

Convergent: narrowing the focus down to the most impactful ideas, so we can actually execute them. This is your *Integrator*.

Resolving those differences in thinking can be very painful. First, the ideas expand like a crescendo (<). And then the ideas are narrowed back into focus, as a composer might call a decrescendo (>). This cycle repeats. Cutting back is super painful for you. For your Integrator, it's super painful to keep dealing with all your ideas. And it's actually pretty painful for any other people who happen to be watching it all unfold. But the push and pull needs to happen.

The Diamond of Creativity[IP]

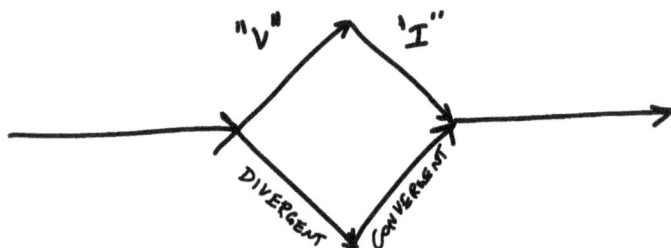

THE DIAMOND OF CREATIVITY

"V"   "I"

DIVERGENT   CONVERGENT

— mcw

When I draw the concept on the whiteboard, the two shapes crescendo (<), decrescendo (>) form a diamond. I call it the Diamond of Creativity because that's the shape it forms and because it is formed through a crucible of pressure and pain. The result is extremely valuable for your business, which is why you're willing to suffer through the pain. At an organizational level, it's great because you really need both types of thinking. We're simply wired differently. And that's okay. We need both sides of the equation.

To take this idea further, you're going to repeat that cycle again and again. You'll be connecting those diamonds together over time. That string of diamonds creates a necklace—the Diamond Necklace of Creativity™—which is even more valuable than the individual stones; it's another superpower of your V/I Duo.

THE DIAMOND NECKLACE

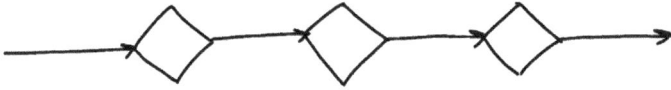

— mcw

The Diamond Necklace of Creativity™

That said, you have to be aware that the process is going to be uncomfortable, at times, for both of you. When you understand that, you'll learn to embrace it. Do your part. Let them do their part. That's the crucible in which your best ideas will be formed, together.

Transformation

On the Think About What You Think About exercise below, you'll see the Seven Mindsets listed. Rate each mindset in terms of importance. The scale is 1–10, with 10 being the most important to you. Then rate how well you feel you're currently doing in each mindset.

MINDSET	IMPORTANCE (1–10)	PERFORMANCE (1–10)
PATIENCE: Being patient when/where necessary?		
OUT TO PASTURE: Feeling creatively engaged and freed, vs simply put "out to pasture"?		
GRATITUDE: Actively focusing on what's good—especially when it's hard?		
INTELLECTUAL HUMILITY: More focused on learning what's right than proving you're right?		
TRUST VS CONTROL: More focused on building V/I trust vs. a need to always be in control?		
GUIDANCE WITHOUT TAMPERING: Driving direction via same page meetings, and leadership team meetings vs. tampering across the organization?		
DIVERGENT THINKING: Embracing my role as a divergent thinker in the creative process, in partnership with the Integrator's need for focus, so they can execute?		

Once you've scored them all, identify the mindset where you have the biggest gap. Find your biggest opportunity and circle it. This should be the mindset that's important to you, and also where you're not currently doing very well.

Make sure to highlight any areas you'd like to discuss in the Community.

VisionaryBook.com

Pillar 6: Think About What You Think About

- ☐ Intentionally shifts their thoughts away from things that are harmful, toward things that are helpful.
- ☐ Demonstrates patience, especially in moments of uncertainty, challenge, or transition.
- ☐ Avoids Out to Pasture thinking. Instead chooses to stay engaged and relevant.
- ☐ Cultivates an attitude of gratitude.
- ☐ Embraces intellectual humility, remaining open to learn and discover different perspectives.
- ☐ Chooses to develop a foundation of trust (vs. control), especially with the Integrator.
- ☐ Provides guidance without tampering, giving direction while honoring others' accountability.
- ☐ Blends their divergent thinking with the integrator's convergent thinking, effectively converting valuable ideas into execution.

To round out this pillar, review your Visionary Report Card (VRC) and read the mindsets above that go along with Pillar 6. Give yourself Xs or slashes next to the mindsets you're doing well in, leaving blank the mindsets where you have substantial work to do. Then give yourself a rating on how well you are doing. The scale is 1–10, with 10 being the highest.

Up next: Pillar 7, Watch Out for Pitfalls.

PILLAR 7

WATCH OUT FOR PITFALLS

In football, as in life, the hits you don't see coming
are the ones that do the most damage.
—*Stuart Scott,* Everyday I Fight

As we move into Pillar 7, I think of a scene from *Raiders of the Lost Ark*. Indiana Jones throws a torch down into a pit and sees it's full of snakes. The only creatures on the planet that disrupt Indy's ultra-cool demeanor. His buddy Salah looks more closely down into the darkness. Taking in what he sees, he turns to Indy, "The floor it moves... asps... very dangerous. You go first."

Dangerous pitfalls are waiting for you, scattered all along your journey. You must be alert. If you know to expect them, you can prepare for them. Step around them. Hop over them. Or get somebody else (maybe a competitor) to go first!

What are these pitfalls we must avoid? Some we've already discussed, so they'll sound familiar to you. And many of them, it turns out, are self-created to some extent. Perhaps the most dangerous pitfalls strangely seem to come from somewhere inside us.

Bad Behavior

One of the most common pitfalls for Visionaries is what I simply call *bad behavior*. This includes tampering, making end runs, undermining your Integrator in front of others, or playing the "Owner's Card."

At some point, you'll likely feel the urge to slip into one or all of these patterns. It's tempting. But here's the truth: these behaviors are toxic. They erode trust, confuse your team, and create a slow drip of distraction, frustration, and wasted energy. The short-term emotional payoff? Not worth the long-term cost to you or the business. And the odds are, this business is the single largest asset in your financial portfolio. Am I right?

The key is awareness. First, recognize that these are *bad behaviors*. Then, learn to spot them quickly, ideally *before* they happen. Anticipate your triggers. Build new habits. Remember that you're better than that. And you're certainly strong enough to rise above the urge. Avoiding this pitfall protects your leadership, your Integrator relationship, and your company's momentum.

Rob was a classic Visionary and had a strong Integrator running the show. One day, Rob bypassed him and gave new marching orders directly to the ops team. It confused everyone, undercut the Integrator's authority, and derailed a project they'd spent weeks aligning on. When I asked Rob why he did it, he said,

"I just got impatient." That one moment of tampering set them back months. The team lost confidence. The Integrator nearly quit. Rob learned the hard way: one emotional impulse can cost far more than it's worth.

Imposter Syndrome

Have you ever felt like an imposter before? Most Visionaries admit that at some point they've experienced this feeling. I know I have.

You develop a sense that everyone else believes you have all the answers. Meanwhile, you sometimes feel unsure that you even know what you're doing. You begin to feel inadequate. Your confidence begins to fall. If you're not confident, how can you instill confidence in your team?

Then this fear creeps in on you. "If they find out that I don't have all the answers, they'll think I'm a fraud. I'll lose all of my credibility!"

Sound familiar?

Let me reassure you that this feeling is normal. Becoming aware of it is the first step toward remedying it.

Reframe your thinking, just like you learned in Pillar 6. Notice when negative thoughts arise and consciously replace them with a positive thought. For example, instead of thinking, "I have no idea what I'm doing," remind yourself, "I've started from scratch before, and I have a track record of figuring things out."

Next, use Pillar 3 and get support. The 7 Posts and the 7 Special Forces form your shield wall. Lean on those trusted relationships to help you navigate these waters. They see your greatness even when you don't.

Finally, give yourself a break! Nobody knows it all. And you probably know much more than you even realize. So don't let this imposter feeling drag you down.

However, you must be proactive about protecting your confidence for your own good and for the business. Dedicate yourself to the Clarity Break discipline we outlined in Pillar 2. Combine your awareness of this pitfall with reframing, support, and a little compassion for yourself. You'll build lasting confidence in your abilities.

A few years ago, I worked with a Visionary who had built a successful company from nothing. Let's call him Jake. On the outside, he was crushing it: company growing, team expanding, press coverage rolling in. But in one of our sessions, he leaned forward, lowered his voice, and said, "I feel like I'm making it all up. Every time someone calls me a genius, I want to run and hide."

So we paused everything else and walked through it. First, I reminded him that this emotion is normal. Most Visionaries hit this point. Then we reframed it. Instead of trying to be the person with all the answers, I challenged him to be the person who asks the right questions and brings the right people along to help. That's what Visionaries do. That's what *he* had always done.

We mapped his track record. We reviewed the wins. We identified key relationships he could lean on. And most importantly, I told him: "They don't follow you because you're perfect. They follow you because you're real, and because you move forward anyway."

Jake didn't fix the feeling overnight. But the shift started there. He started using his Clarity Breaks to name those fears and replaced them with the truth of who he really was. His confidence returned. And his team never left because they believed in him, even when he didn't believe in himself.

Feeling Put Out to Pasture

As we covered in Pillar 6, this is the trap of feeling irrelevant after you've successfully climbed out of the weeds. You've handed off most of the day-to-day, and instead of feeling liberated, you feel unmoored. Like you're drifting without value.

It's a mental trick. You're not being sidelined. You've been repositioned to focus on the highest-value Visionary work only you can do. Staying connected through weekly Level 10s, Same Page Meetings, and regular Scorecard reviews keeps you in the loop.

Think of it like moving from the engine room to the captain's bridge. It's quieter. Less chaotic. At first, it can feel like you're not "doing" anything. But you're actually steering the ship.

Recognize the feeling early and reframe it. That's how you keep from sliding into disengagement. Keep your creativity at the helm, where it belongs.

Becoming the Bottleneck

I see this one a lot. All eyes are on the Visionary. Every decision has to go through you. You have to sign off on everything, all the way down to the little bitty stuff. Yet your involvement in all these decisions slows everything down.

How does this situation evolve? How do you get to such a place?

Recall the way things were when you started the company. Back then, you *had* to do it all yourself. But as the business grew, you didn't let go of much. Maybe you've let go of some details, but nothing of significance. As you've grown, the approaches that used to work for you simply don't work any longer. And as a result, you have become the bottleneck.

So what's a bottleneck? In the *Theory of Constraints*, it's the point that limits a system's total output. Complexity theory calls it a choke point that slows the whole process because everything must pass through it.

Eli Goldratt's *The Goal* defines the game as a constant cycle of finding and fixing bottlenecks to maximize "throughput"—the rate at which your business generates money. Solve one bottleneck, and another will always appear somewhere else.

When a Visionary centralizes all decisions, they create a hub-and-spoke system where they become the constraint. Everything must pass through them. Work slows, decisions back up, and other parts of the business sit idle.

The fix? Identify the bottleneck, then clear it. Delegate decision authority, streamline processes, and empower others to act without waiting for you.

How do you do this? The answer also goes back to Pillar 6: a mindset of Trust vs. Control. A lack of trust in others keeps you from letting go soon enough. You might catch yourself thinking, "I probably don't have the right people. I haven't done the work. We're not aligned." Whatever your reason, you must probe what's going on underneath those feelings.

Open yourself to solving those gaps. Choose people you can trust. Invest time with them to build it. Set crystal-clear expectations. Delegate to people who are wired for the task, having both desire and capability. Then follow up to ensure success. Inspect what you expect. You control each of these steps, so do the work to ensure others are getting done what you used to do.

I once worked with a Visionary we'll call Lisa, who built a thriving consumer brand from scratch. She was brilliant—full of ideas, passionate about the brand, and deeply committed to her team. But as the business grew, her team grew frustrated. Projects slowed down. Decisions piled up in her inbox. Everyone was waiting on Lisa.

She didn't mean to slow things down. She just hadn't realized how much she was still holding onto. Every proposal, every hire, even minor design tweaks had to go through her. When we mapped it out, it was clear: Lisa had become the bottleneck.

We started small. She picked one area—marketing copy—and delegated it fully to her team, with clear expectations and checkpoints. It worked. That freed her up, restored momentum, and gave her the confidence to let go of more. Within a few months, her team was moving faster. Her stress dropped. And her time shifted back toward the big-picture work only *she* could do.

The takeaway? You can be your business's rocket fuel or its cork. It all depends on whether you're willing to let go and trust others to carry the load. Don't let yourself become the bottleneck. It's so easy to do, particularly as your company really starts to grow. Focus on whatever needs to happen to remove yourself as the ultimate constraint on your organization.

Isolation and Loneliness

When you fully inhabit the Visionary seat, you'll notice the game changes. People won't talk to you about the same stuff. They won't talk to you in the same way.

For your part, you may not feel that you can share certain things that are on your mind. You don't want to scare people or come across like a braggart. So you keep these unspoken thoughts to yourself. These thoughts gnaw at you, leading to a feeling of isolation.

Be aware of this, and proactively work to address it. Otherwise, this feeling can lead you to a very dark place.

Lean on the 10 Pillars to support you—that's what they're for! Your V/I counterpart. Your peer group. The people you choose to surround you. Each of these will remind you that "you are not alone."

One Visionary I worked with—let's call him David— ran a wildly successful tech company. From the outside, it looked like he had it all figured out. Inside? He was quietly unraveling. He confided in me one day, "I feel like I'm on an island. Everyone looks to me for answers, but no one really knows the load I'm carrying around."

What changed? David had grown so focused on leading *for* everyone else that he stopped connecting *with* anyone. His team filtered their words around him. Friends couldn't relate. And he didn't feel like he could open up without either freaking people out or sounding arrogant. Consequently, he kept it all inside.

We put a few things in motion. He recommitted to his Integrator relationship and got real with them about what he was feeling in the area of trust. He joined a new peer group of people at his level who faced similar pressures. He even set a weekly "head check" call with a trusted advisor, just to talk out loud and not carry everything alone.

The result? He slowly regained his sense of balance. The isolation lifted. The weight didn't disappear, but now he felt he finally had people helping him carry it.

Being a Visionary doesn't mean being invincible. It means you *feel everything more.* That's why it's critical to surround yourself with the right people who remind you that you're not crazy and you're not alone.

Bounce or Thud?

There's another pattern I've noticed in entrepreneurs, especially when the pressure hits or the bottom drops out. I call it "bounce."

Something big happens: A crisis. A collapse. A global shock, like COVID. The business landscape changes overnight, and suddenly everything feels uncertain. Some entrepreneurs hit the ground hard and *thud.* They're frozen, overwhelmed, done. But others hit the same ground and bounce. They adapt, regroup, and move again, sometimes stronger than before.

Why? It's not luck. It's not superhuman resilience. It's preparation and mindset. It's having the right support, the right disciplines, and the right people *before* the hit comes.

This is why Pitfall Awareness matters. You won't always see the disaster coming, but you can strengthen your foundation in advance. Lean on your tools from the other Pillars: Clarity, Structure, Trust, Support, Spirit. These aren't just tools to optimize your business. They're shock absorbers. They increase your bounce factor.

Imagine you've dropped a rubber ball and a glass ornament from the same height. The fall is the same. The impact is the same. But the outcome is wildly different. One shatters. One bounces. The difference isn't what happens *to* them; it's what they're *made* of.

As a Visionary, you don't control the drop. But you do control what you're made of. You build for bounce[IP] by reinforcing your foundation: clear personal vision, trusted support, and the right mindset. These are the materials that keep you intact—and help you rebound—whenever the next hit comes.

In early 2020, two Visionaries owned restaurants in thriving locations, and both had built strong followings over years of hard work.

Then COVID-19 hit.

One of them—Mike—was paralyzed by fear. He spent weeks waiting for things to "go back to normal." He kept his team on hold, delayed decisions, and hoped the shutdown would blow over. It didn't. By summer, he was out of cash, out of options, and out of the game.

Jess, however, reacted differently. Within forty-eight hours, she'd pivoted to curbside pickup. A week later, she launched meal kits and virtual cooking classes. She called her suppliers, renegotiated terms, and reworked her staff roles. The business didn't just survive, it evolved. And by the time indoor dining returned, she had a stronger model and a broader customer base than before.

What was the difference? Jess *bounced*. Not because she saw the crash coming, but because she'd built the habits, relationships, and mindset that made her ready to adapt. She'd invested in her team. Built systems. Kept herself in a healthy mental space. And trusted her

Integrator to help execute fast. She didn't thud—she rebounded.

You don't control the fall. But you do control how ready you are when it comes.

Build for bounce.

Transformation

On the Watch Out For Pitfalls exercise below, you'll see each of the pitfalls we discussed. First, score your risk of falling into each trap. The scale is 1–10, with 10 being the most risky for you.

PITFALL	RISK (1–10)	MITIGATION STRATEGY
BAD BEHAVIOR		
FEELING PUT OUT TO PASTURE		
IMPOSTER SYNDROME		
BECOMING THE BOTTLENECK		
ISOLATION / LONELINESS		
BOUNCE OR THUD?		

Once you've scored them all, identify the pitfall where you have the biggest risk. Think of some ways that you could proactively work to avoid or mitigate that risk. Write those down. And make sure to highlight any areas you'd like to discuss in the Community.

Pillar 7: Watch For Pitfalls

☐ Avoids bad behavior (tampering, end runs, playing the owner card, etc.).

☐ No longer feels put Out to Pasture. Embraces their intrinsic genius.

☐ Avoids Imposter Syndrome. Recognizes they've earned the right to be where they are.

☐ Avoids becoming the bottleneck. Knows when and where to let go.

☐ Avoids isolation. Knows they are not alone.

☐ Seeks support early. Uses personal warning signs to recognize and stop harmful behaviors before they cause damage.

To round out this pillar, review your Visionary Report Card (VRC) for the mindsets above that go along with Pillar Seven. Give yourself Xs or slashes next to the mindsets you're doing well in, leaving blank the mindsets where you have substantial work to do. Then give yourself a rating on how well you are doing overall. The scale is 1–10, with 10 being the highest.

Up next: Pillar 8: Help Others Stretch.

PILLAR 8

HELP OTHERS STRETCH

A mind that is stretched by a new experience can
never go back to its old dimensions.
—*Oliver Wendell Holmes Jr.*

Bill Gates said, "Most people overestimate what they can do in one year—and underestimate what they can do in ten years." This idea stems from Amara's Law, which states: We tend to overestimate the effect of technology in the short run—and underestimate it in the long run. Roy Amara was a futurist with degrees from Stanford, Harvard, and MIT—a pretty bright guy. His principle highlights how business leaders often fall into this trap on both ends of the time horizon. We expect more than what is possible this quarter/year, and yet we sell short our ambition for what we could actually achieve in this decade. I've watched leadership planning play out in this instinctive thinking pattern so many times,

I've literally lost count. And, admittedly, I've also been guilty of this.

An unrealistic short-term plan drives frustration, burnout, turnover, and often poorly informed decision-making that can tangibly harm the firm. If the numbers are never hit, they become meaningless. Incurring expenses on the promise of revenue that doesn't materialize is a recipe for failure. Who wants to play for a team that never wins?

Likewise, any long-term plans depend on taking action in the present, even if it's just getting more clear on the path forward. At some point, you must start by taking initial steps toward that vision. If you don't, and continue "kicking the can" down the road, you'll never realize the opportunity that was actually there.

Meaningful changes to your organization, whether they involve technology or not, can be transformative. Arguably, the human energy in your business is still the most powerful force at your command. As Visionaries, we need to encourage our team to stretch in a healthy way. What does healthy mean in this context? Well, let's start by looking at what "unhealthy" is.

Someone in the organization says, "We haven't hit our numbers in years. They're always so far out there. They're impossible to hit."

Then somebody, usually the Visionary, says, "Yeah, but we're going to shoot for the stars and land on the moon."

This "stretching" notion dominates every single priority they set—regardless of time span. And the team always falls short, in spite of their great efforts. The team becomes demoralized. And because of these bad predictions, poor decisions are made.

That's not the healthy stretching we seek.

The Vision Tree™

To help your team stretch without snapping, you must root them in reality while inviting them to reach for possibility. My friend, Mark Abbott, Founder of Ninety. io, says, "If your vision isn't rooted in something achievable, it's not inspiring—it's misleading."

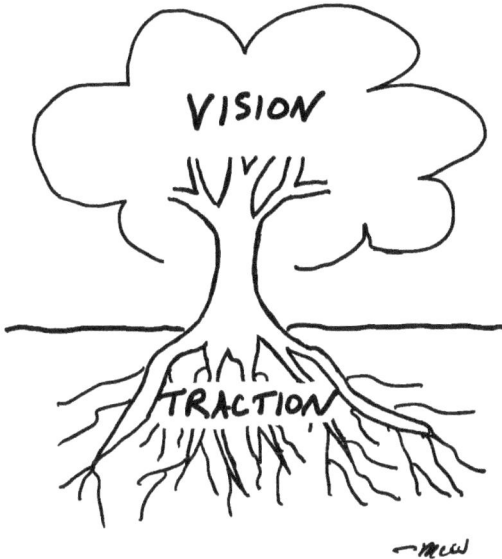

THE VISION TREE

VISION

TRACTION

Think of it like a tree: The roots are your traction— grounded, predictable, and disciplined. The branches are your vision—expansive, inspiring, and unconstrained.

If the tree stretches too far without roots, it topples. If the roots are deep but there's no stretch, it stagnates. Healthy stretch lives in the tension between the two.

Healthy Stretching with the V/TO®

It turns out, the EOS process is perfect for both sides of your Visionary brain. What I mean by that is: while you need to stretch, you also need to predict. The Vision/Traction Organizer® (V/TO) is a powerful tool in this regard. Go to our Resource Page for a link to download the V/TO and more free tools inside the EOS Academy.

VisionaryBook.com

It's a two-page strategic planning tool that simplifies and clarifies your company's vision by answering eight key questions. The Vision side captures your long-term vision (beyond one year), while the Traction side captures your near-term plan (within one year). It aligns your leadership team on who you are, where you're going, and how you'll get there by bringing focus and discipline to your execution. The V/TO creates a clear roadmap to achieve your vision with traction.

Vision is where we stretch.
Traction is where we predict.

Vision is where we stretch. Traction is where we predict.

As I tell my clients, look at the way the V/TO is set up. Vision on one side. Traction on the other. We predict on the Traction side. When you are planning inside of twelve months, you need to predict the most impactful initiatives and outcomes for the overall year and the upcoming quarter. In other words, your One-Year Plan and your 90-Day Rocks. You "call your shot" as close as you can to what's actually going to happen. Don't overshoot it. Don't stretch. Likewise, don't dramatically undershoot it and be a "sandbagger."

To become an effective leadership team, we ask you to become excellent predictors. Remember, ninety days goes by quickly. If you don't already know most of the "how" for an initiative, getting it done will often take longer than you realize. Any time there are unknowns involved, an alarm bell should go off inside your head that warns you to dial back your prediction. Accountability for achieving the Rocks at the end of each quarter will teach you this lesson in short order. *Don't overreach*. The more you know the "how," the more aggressive you can be with your predictions. If this is an area where you have lots of experience, you may feel very confident versus someone who has little or no experience with the same area. If you're not at least 80 percent sure, it's not really a prediction. It's a stretch.

Healthy stretching means that you stretch *and* you predict. Stretching your team in a healthy way is motivating and aligning. It's challenging them to think differently about how they're seeing things today. You stretch on the Vision side of the V/TO. The two best areas to stretch your thinking are the 10-Year Target and 3-Year Picture. Here's an example:

When you're setting the 10-Year Target on the V/TO, you're looking far out on the horizon. The business landscape will look very different ten years from now, but you don't need to predict all of that. We're trying to name a target out there that resonates with us. One that has meaning and we can anchor into that distant horizon. You want to plant a flag that everyone in the company can see off in the distance. If you do a good job, it energizes your people in three powerful ways.

- First, it's attractive and motivating. You want it. You're drawn toward it. You're driven to take the steps necessary to make it happen.
- Second, it aligns the leadership. Instead of your leadership team being pointed in five different directions, they're all pointed toward this single point on the horizon. You generate tremendous power when all that human energy is focused in a single direction.

    Think of it like sunlight. Scattered light warms things up. But focused through a lens, that same sunlight can ignite fire. That's the power of focused human energy.
- Finally, it challenges you to think differently about how you're approaching things today. Realizing that you want that future, you then take a harder look at how things are operating today and shake your head. You can see that you'll never reach that future if you keep doing things the same way as they're being done today. In turn, that triggers you to stretch your thinking in the present. What's missing? What needs

to change? What must we get rid of in order for us to line up with the trajectory that takes us to this future that you've said you want?

Stretch vs. Predict: A Visionary Dilemma

As a Visionary, possibility is your superpower. But your leadership team runs more on probability. They need to believe the future you describe *could* happen, and they need to know what to do next. That's the art of Healthy Stretching.

You stretch their imagination toward the long-term vision.

You predict with discipline in the short term to build credibility. Growing strong roots at the base of your Vision Tree.

When you do both well, your team will follow you anywhere. But if you blur the line—stretching where you should predict, or failing to cast vision at all—you risk disengagement, burnout, or stagnation.

The question becomes: How far is too far to stretch? That's what led me to create the Vision Expander Tool[IP].

Vision Expander Tool™

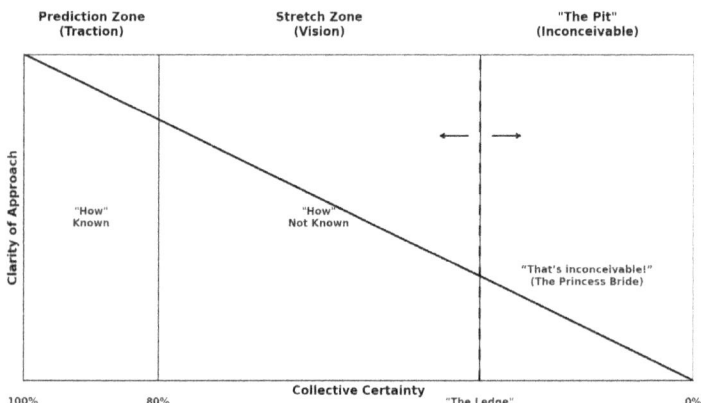

| Prediction Zone (Traction) | Stretch Zone (Vision) | "The Pit" (Inconceivable) |

So how much do you stretch?

Here's how I'll explain it. Think about a gauge of certainty that goes from 100 percent down to 0 percent, divided into three zones.

One end of the gauge is the prediction zone. Anything listed here is 80–100 percent certain. We are confident we can make those changes happen because we know precisely how we're going to do it. We may even have done something very similar before. These are the goals in your 1-Year Plan and your 90-Day Rocks—both on the Traction side of your V/TO.

Once you venture past the 80 percent line, you've moved into the "stretch zone." Your level of certainty is falling. Maybe you're at 70 percent, or 60 percent, or less. You no longer see clearly how to pull it off, or at least not all of it. Once you drop below 50 percent certain, you're really stretching. A lot of questions about how to go forward are unanswered. You'll likely have to invent a lot of steps to make the objective happen. The farther you go, you keep getting less and less certain. Somewhere over there, as the certainty drops, you cross another line that I call the Ledge of Conceivability™. Remember our Vision Tree? Think of this as the leaves on the farthest branches.

Over on the left side of the ledge, it's conceivable that you can figure it out. You don't know how, at least not all of how, but you have some relevant prior experience that is giving you confidence. Maybe you're saying to yourself, "If all the stars align, it's conceivable to me that we could figure out how to make it happen."

Now you've stretched all the way to the limits of your conceivability. Your toes are hanging off the Ledge there. Can you picture it? Kinda scary, right?

The third zone is just past that Ledge of Conceivability. If you take one more step beyond that Ledge, guess what's there? Yep, it's the "pit of inconceivability" (for all you *Princess Bride* fans out there). Down in the pit, you don't believe we can do it. It's inconceivable to you. As a result, you simply don't give it much more thought.

What happens if you drag your people off that ledge? They'll end up down there in the pit, and they'll groan, "This is stupid...we can't do this. What an idiot! This is just such a waste. This is such an exercise of futility." Their brains will check out. That is to say, they'll do what you tell them. They'll still collect their paycheck. But you've now lost 80–90 percent of their creative power!

Meanwhile, if we stretch all the way to the ledge, without going over, it's a very different place. Imagine the whole team perched there on the edge of the ledge, with toes hanging off—it's exciting and tingly. Something magical happens. The goal is still conceivable. Their brain engages. "Well, I don't know exactly how we'll do this, but I think we might be able to get there." Their brain goes into a problem-solving mode to figure it out. They start asking, "How could we do it? What do we have to change? What do we have to stop? What gap do we have to close to make this happen?" A team of people thinking together like this creates a multiplier effect. You start to come up with some really cool ideas that you can bat around. They end up in your short-term thinking, as practical steps on the trajectory toward that future.

Your Role as Visionary

That's the kind of stretching that you need to get your team to do. They won't naturally make that leap.

Using the 10-Year Target as an example, you might decide to pursue a revenue number. It will be an indicator of growth that you can easily hang your narrative around. You can imagine a growth story that brings a boatload of opportunities for your people: professional growth, skill development, new experiences, market recognition, community impact, geographic mobility, and financial rewards. Once you've agreed on that as meaningful, you naturally move to the question of how much revenue in that year or ten years from now. Remind everyone to "stretch to the ledge." Everyone gives it some thought on their own and writes down a number. We quickly go around the table to hear each person's idea: 50. 60. 75. 70. 70.

If we start with the lowest number, 50, the question to this leader is, "Why not higher? And there's no judgment here." You'll get some insight into their thinking. You also might challenge them gently. "So, 55 is inconceivable for you? No way that could happen?" In my experience, they'll often say, "No, that's not inconceivable." At this point, someone else might propose an idea that nobody else had considered, which moves everyone higher. Keep pushing to see where their top line really is. That's how you'll land on a number that is exciting for all, and still conceivable for all.

Steve Jobs was famously said to possess a "reality distortion field"—a term originally used by his colleagues at Apple. It described his uncanny ability to convince others (and perhaps even himself) that the impossible was not only possible, but inevitable. Under its influence, engineers would commit to absurd deadlines. Designers would push past what they thought were their limits. People would achieve things they never believed they could—simply because Jobs insisted they could.

This trait, at its best, is a powerful part of the Visionary's role. The Visionary sees things others can't yet see, and believes in a version of the future that doesn't exist yet. That belief can be contagious. It pulls people forward. It elevates performance. It breaks through constraints. But like any superpower, it comes with a dark side: if untethered from reality, it can lead to exhaustion, disillusionment, and breakdown. The key is not to eliminate the distortion, but to *harness it with intention*. When combined with clear short-term grounding, like the prediction discipline for anything within the next twelve months, a well-directed Reality

Distortion Field becomes a force that builds legendary teams, products, and companies.

The great Visionary will inspire this discussion. You just throw out an idea: "We could do this, or build this, or acquire this." The team may realize: "I never thought about that!" You'll end up discovering that space where stretching is exciting for everyone, and still conceivable to all. It's the space that engages all that creative juice and really gets them going.

This is what helping others stretch—in a healthy way—is all about. We need you to help others stretch where they should. Stretch the Vision. Predict the Traction. You must do both. The result is a leadership team that is challenged, aligned, engaged, and motivated.

Transformation

For this exercise, refer to your current V/TO as you work through the table below.

	CERTAINTY (0–100%)	NOTES
VISION		
10-YEAR TARGET		
3-YEAR PICTURE		
TRACTION		
1-YEAR PLAN		
90-DAY ROCKS		

How "stretchy" is your Vision? How certain are you about your 10-Year Target? Is it really stretchy? Are you on the ledge, or can you already see most of the "how"?

Same thing for your 3-Year Picture. How certain are you? How predictive is your plan?

Then, think about the Goals in your 1-Year Plan. What's your confidence level that you're going to be able to accomplish those? Are you predicting, or stretching? Be honest with yourself.

How about the current Rocks that you have in place—your biggest priorities? What's your confidence level that you'll get those done?

Put a number on it. From 0–100 percent, where 0 percent is "not a chance we get there" and 100 percent is "not a chance we don't get there."

Write down your percentages, then write down some notes about how each feels for you at this moment. Reflect on how we described healthy stretching on the Vision side and well-disciplined predicting on the Traction side.

Are you stretching the Vision?

Are you predicting the Traction?

Don't overthink this. Go with what your gut is telling you. And make sure to highlight any areas you'd like to discuss in the Community.

Pillar 8: Help Others Stretch

- ☐ Stretches others to the Ledge of Conceivability, not by pushing harder, but by expanding belief.
- ☐ Balances aspiration with clarity; stretches just far enough to inspire, without overreaching.
- ☐ Ensures that the long-term vision is grounded in reality, but not constrained by it.
- ☐ Ensures everyone understands and supports the 10-Year Target.
- ☐ Embraces the discipline of prediction; sets clear targets with 80 percent confidence on the Traction side of the plan.
- ☐ Inspires others with big ideas, then partners with the Integrator to bring them down to earth.

To round out this pillar, review your Visionary Report Card (VRC) about the mindsets above that go along with Pillar 8. Give yourself Xs or slashes next to the mindsets you're doing well in, leaving blank the mindsets where you have substantial work to do. Then give yourself a rating on how well you are doing overall. The scale is 1–10, with 10 being the highest.

Up next: Pillar 9: Go Slow to Go Fast.

PILLAR 9
GO SLOW TO GO FAST

Slow is smooth, smooth is fast.

—*US Navy SEALs*

The Visionary Tension

Most Visionaries hate the idea of slowing down. Scratch that. Almost every Visionary I've ever met is resistant to slowing down.

Why? It feels wrong. Unnatural. Wasteful. Even dangerous.

But here's the truth: if you never slow down, you will crash your business or your life.

I've seen it over and over. Visionaries push at full throttle, then wonder why the team is confused, systems are breaking, and progress stalls.

The irony is that slowing down is often the fastest way to get where you actually want to go. When you pause to clarify your vision, think deeply, reset priorities, communicate, or make a high-leverage decision, you create alignment. And alignment creates velocity.

Going fast without alignment is wasted energy.

But when everything and everyone is pointed in the same direction? Now you're moving. Fast. Clean. Powerfully.

If you don't go slow *on purpose*, you'll eventually go slow *by force*.

Before we get into the mechanics of how to slow down, I want to share a story that brings this principle to life. It's a lesson I learned secondhand. And it's one I'll never forget. It captures exactly why pacing yourself matters more than you think.

Slow to Survive

My good friend and fellow Expert EOS Implementer, Alex Freytag, takes periodic "clarity trips." An extended trip away, often someplace rather epic, to get crystal clear and totally realigned. One time, Alex's clarity trip was to climb Mount Kilimanjaro. As he shared the story afterward, a particular nugget of wisdom stuck with me.

The guides had one repeated instruction:

"Poli! Poli!"

It means "slowly, slowly" in Swahili.

That was their strategy. Not because they weren't strong or fast, but because they understood what was at stake. The higher the altitude, the greater the risk. Push too fast and you get altitude sickness. You burn out. You break down. You go back down. You fail to reach the summit.

Poli! Poli! is how you reach the summit.

Jim Collins famously calls this the Twenty Mile March. A consistent, sustainable pace no matter the conditions. Whether it's sunny or stormy, whether you feel like it or not, you march your twenty miles. Not ten. Not fifty. Twenty.

It's not about bursts of genius. It's about rhythm, endurance, and intent—measured movement toward a long-term goal. That's how great companies thrive. And it's how great Visionaries stay in the game long enough to win.

So when the urge hits to sprint ahead, remember: Slow is smooth. Smooth is fast. And sometimes, not always, slow is about survival.

The lesson from Kilimanjaro is clear: survival, success, and speed all start with the right pace. And I learned that same truth in a very different setting—face down in a swimming pool, gasping for air.

Slow Is Smooth, Smooth Is Fast

That odd phrase comes from a personal experience back when I was doing triathlons. Swim. Bike. Run. Of the three, swimming was by far my weakest, so I got a swim coach.

During my first session, the coach noticed something immediately. My fitness from running and biking did *not* translate to the water. And I had only one setting— max effort.

In the middle of a lap, he stopped me and shouted, "Slow is smooth. Smooth is fast." I shot back, "That makes no sense!"

He explained that when you slow down in the water, you reduce drag. You eliminate wasted motion, creating less friction and expending less energy. You glide. That's what makes you faster.

The harder you fight the water, the more it fights you back. When you slow down and smooth it out, you actually do move faster and conserve energy.

The same applies to Visionaries.

When your energy is erratic and all over the place, it creates drag. Confusion. Misalignment. Negativity ripples throughout your team.

But when your movements are smooth and intentional, everything flows. Everyone around you can follow and contribute. Friction goes down. Progress speeds up.

Slow is smooth. Smooth is fast. It's not just a swimming tip; it's a leadership principle.

What's really happening when we slow down? Underneath the surface, it's all about changing the kind of energy you put into your team and your company. That shift away from frantic motion and toward deliberate movement is the difference between friction and flow.

Friction vs. Flow

Your energy doesn't exist in a vacuum. People feel it. React to it. Mirror it.

When that energy is chaotic—rushed, disorganized, reactive—it creates friction. Friction burns energy, slows progress, and derails your momentum.

Your team starts scrambling. Priorities shift. Communication breaks down. And suddenly, what *should've* been simple now takes twice as long.

This is the "hidden tax" on Visionary chaos.

But here's the good news: the opposite is also true.

When your energy is focused and steady, calm, and deliberate, it creates flow. Flow reduces drag. It lifts people and aligns effort. It clears the path forward. Your leadership becomes a tailwind instead of a headwind.

And the result? Your team moves faster, smarter, and with less waste.

If you want to go fast, don't just push harder. Eliminate the friction. Smooth the energy, and let the flow do its work.

One of the fastest ways to move from friction to flow is to narrow your attention. As a Visionary, your energy is like sunlight. Powerful but often too scattered to have real impact. That's where focus comes in.

Focus

Focus is your first tool for eliminating friction and generating smooth energy.

But here's the challenge: your natural state as a Visionary is often scattered. You're overflowing with ideas. Excited by what's next. Pulled toward what's new.

It feels productive, but it's actually a trap. If you focus on everything, you focus on nothing.

That's why we limit your Rocks. I push leadership teams to have five or fewer for the company, with the individual leaders taking no more than three. From there, if we can simply have everyone else in the company setting and completing one great Rock—every single quarter—that's real power. Not because your company isn't capable of taking on more Rocks, but because focus creates force.

Focus means saying *no* to good ideas so you can say, "Hell, yes!" to the right ones. And increase your odds of completion. That's what drives impact.

As a Visionary, you are the sun radiating energy in every direction. But here's the thing:

> The sun provides the Earth with billions of kilowatts of energy, yet if you stand in it for an hour, the worst you will get is a little sunburn. On the other hand, a few watts of energy focused in one direction is all a laser beam needs to cut through diamonds.
>
> —Al Ries, *Focus*

Here's another way to think about it:

Imagine placing a wide board flat on top of a table. Now take a hammer and slam it down, trying to drive that board into the table. What happens? Nothing. The energy gets dispersed across the entire surface area of the board.

Now imagine the same hammer, same table, but this time you're striking a nail. All that energy is concentrated to the point of that nail. And it drives right into the table. Same energy, different focus.

Focus is the difference between wasted effort and real impact.

Bring your energy into focus, as through a magnifying glass. That's when things will ignite.

Remember: choosing *not* to do something might feel slow in the moment. But it's the very thing that lets you go fast later.

When you've got true focus, something powerful starts to happen: you can slip into a state where everything just works. Psychologists call it flow. It's the ultimate force multiplier for a Visionary.

Flow — Your Force Multiplier

Flow is your next lever. And when you get it right, it acts as a multiplier.

Psychologist Mihály Csíkszentmihályi first coined the term in the 1970s to describe that immersive, high-performance mental state where everything just clicks. Time disappears. Energy is created, not consumed. You're locked in.

He called it "flow" because his research subjects kept describing the sensation as being carried effortlessly by a current. One action flows into the next. There's no friction. No wasted motion.

You've felt it. We all have. And you can design your work to create it more often.

Flow isn't just about working harder. It's about creating the conditions for your brain—and your team—to operate at peak performance. Steven Kotler, a leading researcher on the topic, puts it simply: "Flow follows focus."

That's why the previous section matters so much. You can't get into flow when you split your attention in ten directions, or you react to every email, notification, or shiny object that flies across your desk.

You enter flow when you:

- Eliminate distractions.
- Work on something meaningful.

- Match challenge with skill.
- Give your full attention to what's in front of you.

As a Visionary, when *you* enter flow, it's contagious. People around you feel it. Your Integrator feels it. Your company starts moving with rhythm and ease. This is when leadership becomes almost effortless, breakthroughs occur, and momentum builds quickly.

Slow (focus) is smooth (flow). Smooth (flow) is fast (results).

Focus and flow don't mean shutting down your creativity. Your best ideas still need to fly. The trick is knowing when and how to land them.

Let the Ideas Fly, Then Land Them Safely

Here's the paradox: You *shouldn't* slow down your ideas.

Let them come fast. That's part of your Visionary genius. Don't dam the flow. In fact, you want to find ways to encourage that flow of ideas. But just because you dreamed up the idea fast doesn't mean you have to act on it fast. Speed of thought is not the same as speed of implementation.

This is where many Visionaries get in trouble. You get a spark, you voice it, and the team panics. They scramble to build, shift priorities, or kill other projects—all because you were just "thinking out loud." The fix? Separate ideation from activation.

Here's how:

- Create a "Crazy Ideas List." A place where you can capture new ideas as they come. You might share this with your Integrator, but you don't have to.

- Set a regular rhythm—weekly, bi-weekly, or monthly—where you review these "crazy" ideas *together*.
- Use criteria like: "What problem is this solving?" "How urgent is it?" "Is this a Now, Next, or Later?"
- Give your Integrator permission (and encouragement) to challenge each idea's readiness and alignment with the company's vision and plan.

You're not muting your creativity. You're maturing it. And ironically? That's what makes your best ideas stick—and succeed.

And when those ideas do land, not every bit of resistance you encounter is a problem to be eliminated. Some friction is actually your friend. Especially when it comes from the right source.

All Friction Isn't the Enemy

Once the idea is out of your head and into the open, what happens next matters.

Too often, Visionaries treat pushback as resistance. But smart pushback isn't resistance; it's refinement. Especially when it comes from your Integrator.

Your Integrator sees the operational friction you don't: the resourcing issues, how people are impacted, the downstream chaos. That's not negativity. That's their gift that keeps you from driving off a cliff at one hundred miles an hour.

Here's how to *go slow on purpose* in those conversations:

- Signal your intent. Say: "I'm in idea mode—not action mode. Help me think this through."
- Make it safe to disagree. Ask: "Where do you see friction I'm not seeing?"
- Admit your blind spots. "I know I skip steps. What obstacles would trip us up?"
- Let them say no or not yet. And actually listen to them.

You're still the Visionary. You still get to lead. But great leadership doesn't mean pushing every idea through. It means letting your best ideas survive contact with reality.

One of the best places to put this into practice is in the room with your team. Meetings are where pace and process either create clarity or kill it.

Slow Down the Room

Your meetings reveal your speed. If you rush through the agenda, jump in with solutions, or dominate the airspace—guess what? You're teaching the team that speed matters more than clarity. But in reality, speed kills truth.

When your team doesn't feel space to think, reflect, or dissent, they default to agreement. Not alignment. Going fast might get you apparent consensus. But going slow gets you commitment.

Here's how to intentionally slow the room:

- Don't use meetings to convince. Use them to *collaborate*.
- Say, "I want to hear from everyone before we make a call."
- Start with the quietest people first.
- Ask disarming questions like, "What are we missing?" or "What makes you hesitate?"
- Invite people to challenge your ideas without challenging your identity.

Slowing down the room might feel inefficient. But it's not. It's how you surface blind spots, invite ownership, and make better decisions that actually stick.

Now don't get me wrong, not all meetings should move slowly. In

If we go fast where we can, then we can go slow where we should.

fact, there are many things you can do to go fast. Be prepared. Be decisive. Stay engaged. Don't repeat the same points that have already been made. Don't waste the team's time on work that could've been done in advance without them. Keep a healthy tempo, without rushing.

If we go fast where we can, then we can go slow where we should.

If we go slow everywhere, we won't have enough time, much less energy, left to really dive into the things that may need it the most.

If you approach all your meetings like this, they'll never be boring, and they'll always be impactful.

Slowing the pace matters in the conference room. But it matters even more in the most important room you'll ever lead: the one you walk into when you get home.

The Most Important Room

Being a Visionary is a high-speed role. Your mind races. Your energy drives the business. But when you walk through your front door, that same pace doesn't work. Your family doesn't need a CEO. They need *you*. Present, grounded, and unrushed.

Here's how to slow your roll:

- Build a transition ritual. Use your commute, a short walk, or ten quiet minutes to downshift before entering home life.
- Visualize your shift. Imagine taking your foot off the gas—going from "work tempo" to "family cruise."
- Choose a reset cue. A simple reminder like: "This is the most important room I lead."
- Leave the laptop closed. If your attention isn't with your family, your body is simply a placeholder.

Going slow at home doesn't mean you stop caring. It means you start leading differently, at a pace your family can actually connect with.

That's one way you build a life that's worth building a business for.

Even when you know how to slow down in the right moments, it's tempting to speed up everywhere else. That's when you run into a trap I call the Traffic Jam Theory[IP].

The Traffic Jam Theory

You're speeding. You're ambitious. You're trying to make something happen.

But suddenly...you're stuck. Everything's moving slower than you want.

So how do you react? You switch lanes. Then that lane backs up more. You press harder. You swerve. You honk. You get frustrated.

Sound familiar? This is the essence of my Traffic Jam Theory—and it applies directly to your Visionary role.

Sometimes the faster you try to go, the more jammed up everything gets. Why?

You're introducing too many initiatives. Spinning up too many priorities. Distracting your team with new directions before the last ones were even clear.

And your company—like traffic—responds with a slowdown, congestion, and gridlock.

Let's break it down:

- Lane switching = context switching. Every time you shift focus, so does your team. Switching burns time and energy, increases confusion, and rarely gets you ahead.
- Rubbernecking = shiny object syndrome. Technically, you're still moving forward, but your attention is no longer on the destination.
- Phantom jams = self-inflicted chaos. There's no visible cause—just a build-up of minor, unco-ordinated changes, misaligned Rocks, surprise projects, and goal shifts.

- Overloaded on-ramps = too many ideas entering too fast. No metering. No filtering. Just jammed lanes and overwhelmed people.
- Gridlock = Visionary whiplash. So many things are moving in so many directions that nothing actually moves at all.

The solution isn't to swerve harder. It's to create space to finish what's already in motion. Space for people to catch up. Space for timing to shift in your favor.

Sometimes, the smartest move isn't to push forward. It's to pull over. Use that space to recheck the map. Reassess your route to ensure you're still headed where you truly want to go.

- Map = Vision
- GPS recalculating = Same Page Meetings + weekly leadership meetings
- Throttle control = Your energy and urgency
- Instrument panel = Signals from your team you can't afford to ignore

Progress isn't about constant motion. It's about steadily moving forward. And that only happens when you go slow, on purpose.

The Traffic Jam Theory demonstrates that constant motion can make you slower. The shift you need to make is from frenetic to intentional energy.

The Shift from Frenetic to Intentional

At first, slowing down will feel wrong, unnatural. Just like it did for me in the pool. You'll feel like you're giving up momentum. Like you're falling behind or not doing your job as a Visionary.

But that feeling is just your old wiring, your old belief that more speed equals more progress. What you're doing now is different. You're creating intentional energy. You're replacing chaos with clarity and choosing direction over reaction.

Now you're leading.

When you do this well, everything around you changes:

- You replace stress with confidence.
- You replace noise with signal.
- You replace confusion with conviction.

You're no longer the source of friction; instead, you're the trigger for flow.

Your team will feel it, and they'll start showing up differently. Stronger. Clearer. Faster.

You'll need a new mantra:

Slow is Smooth. Smooth is Fast.

And a new formula:

Slow (Focus) → Smooth (Flow) → Fast (Results)

Live it. Model it. Multiply it.

Now lock it in. This isn't theory. It's about seeing exactly where your speed is helping and where it's hurting. Just like on the mountain. Or in the water. The right pace gets you to the finish you seek. Use this quick self-check to spot your biggest friction points. And your best opportunities to create flow.

Transformation

In the exercise below, you'll find several behaviors and traps discussed in this chapter. Start by scoring yourself on each one. Use a 1–10 scale, where 10 means you fall into that pattern frequently and it's costing you momentum, and 1 means it's rare or simply not a problem for you.

Then take a moment to reflect on what's driving your high scores. Is it a habit? Fear of missing out on an opportunity? A team issue? Write down any notes or possible solutions in the Mitigation column.

PATTERN / TRAP	RISK (1–10)	MITIGATION
Running at full throttle all the time		
Pushing ideas into action too quickly		
Constant context switching… "jumping around"		
Starting new before clearing old		
Resisting Integrator feedback		
Rushing meetings or silencing dissent		
Struggling to slow down at home		

Once you've scored them all, identify the pattern where you're at greatest risk. What's one intentional change you could make to reduce that friction and create more space? Write it down. Consider sharing it with your Integrator or in the Community.

Pillar 9: Go Slow to Go Fast

☐ Spots and tames their default frenetic patterns before they kill momentum.

☐ Resets quickly when their own behavior creates unnecessary chaos.

☐ Leverages focus to trigger flow within the team.

☐ Understands the Traffic Jam Theory; works hard to prevent bottlenecks and protect flow.

☐ Slows down on purpose in meetings and at home to get better results.

Finally, review your Visionary Report Card (VRC) for the mindsets above that go along with Pillar 9. Mark the mindsets you're consistently practicing with Xs. Give yourself a slash next to the mindsets you're doing pretty well in. Leave the rest blank as growth opportunities. Then rate your overall performance for this pillar on a scale from 1 to 10, with 10 being the highest. Take a quiet minute now to do the VRC and capture your thoughts.

I'll see you in the next chapter, where we explore Pillar 10: Do No Harm. You're in the home stretch!

PILLAR 10

DO NO HARM

First, do no harm.

—*Hippocratic Oath*

Wow, you made it to Pillar 10! Pretty impressive for a Visionary! (And I'm sure you were never distracted along the way.)

When I was growing up, my dad was a small-town doctor in Poteau, Oklahoma. And, yes, I've heard all the jokes. Anyway, he had a plaque hanging in his office. As a young boy, it was tough for me to read because it was written in a calligraphy-style font. And some of it was in Latin. It was the Hippocratic Oath. One day, I asked him what it meant. He said, "First, do no harm." He continued, "Son, that means that the first rule of being a good doctor is to make sure you don't kill anybody." And he could not have had a more matter-of-fact expression on his face as he delivered that line. Dad always had a great way of simplifying the lesson.

The wisdom of Hippocrates has come down across the ages directly to you, the visionary entrepreneur. As a Visionary, that's really important for you to hear. Do no harm. In your role, the damage isn't physical, but the harm is real. It shows up as lost momentum, broken trust, and burned-out teams.

It is one of the most powerful lessons you can take from this book.

You can do a lot to slow down the whole process and blow the wheels right off the train. We have talked about avoiding bad behavior and discussed tampering. Don't initiate or enable those end runs we talked about earlier. Communicate freely, while working decisions and providing direction through your accountability structure. Those are examples of doing no harm, even when you're itching to lay your hands on a problem you see.

Yet this prescription goes beyond day-to-day business processes. Wisdom lies deeper in your approach to your business. So let's see what lies at the heart of every successful Visionary.

No Vision Confusion

You must not display "vision confusion" or openly talk about alternative visions that conflict with one another. A vision for rapid growth conflicts with a vision for staying small, while a vision for national expansion also likely conflicts with a vision for dominating your local state.

The majority of Visionaries are clear on where they want to go. However, experiencing a lack of clarity can critically debilitate your team. They rapidly lose confidence, lose focus, and may get highly confused. Your organization will begin to leak energy.

- "You said we were going to dominate Texas, period. So why are we opening a new office in Colorado?"
- "To support our growth goal, we'll need those resources we had researched at length and agreed on. So why are all of our new growth investments suddenly being put on hold?"

This is a real problem. You may have become confused yourself. If so, make it a priority to get yourself clear again—ASAP. And don't drag your people through your mental (or perhaps psychological) process of sorting it out. Settle the question for yourself, then bring them back to Vision Clarity.

No Waffling

As a leader, you cannot be noncommittal. For example, don't agree to run on EOS, and then make moves that unwind the progress day after day. Don't agree to the Visionary/Integrator structure, and then fail to abide by the 5 Rules that help make that relationship work. You are creating so much wasted energy when this happens. It's so frustrating for everyone else involved. You are in, or you are out. Either one can work. Decide and commit.

I worked with a company where the Visionary, Lisa, claimed she was "all in" on EOS. She hired a strong Integrator, Tom, rolled out the tools, and started gaining traction. But within a few months, the cracks showed.

Lisa would skip Level 10s, derail Rocks mid-quarter with new ideas, and have side conversations with team members that completely contradicted decisions made in Same Page Meetings.

Tom finally said what the whole team was thinking: "Lisa, are we doing this or not?"

To her credit, Lisa didn't get defensive. She realized her half-in, half-out behavior was eroding trust and killing momentum. So she called a meeting, owned it, and made a clear choice: "We *are* doing this, and I'm going to show it."

From that point on, Lisa stuck to the structure. She followed the meeting pulse, honored the Visionary and Integrator lines of accountability, and stopped chasing shiny objects. The team could finally breathe and perform. And their results quickly showed it.

No Special Exceptions

This is different from being an employee when you're working in the business. No more special exceptions means you can't exempt yourself from the company system you put in place. A typical comment is: "Well, yeah, but I'm me. I don't have to do that." Really? Then why should anyone else do it? When you are unwilling to follow your own rules, it signals your view of importance. A weekly leadership meeting that you regularly attend will naturally be viewed as much more important than one that you rarely make a priority to attend.

No special exceptions for others either. Those exceptions sound like, "This is my son, or my spouse, or my good friend, or my person that's been with me since day one, so they have a special exception." I once held a Quarterly session where the Visionary's daughter had recently joined the company's sales team. There was clearly an issue related to the daughter, and the Sales leader was trying to raise it for discussion. It was getting visibly uncomfortable for the Visionary, and he tried to deflect attention from the issue. As an experienced EOS Implementer, I smelled a deeper issue that really needed to be explored.

At EOS Worldwide, "Do the Right Thing" is a Core Value. Part of what that means is that we must be willing to "Enter the Danger." In this case, we must lead a client into a place they need to go, even when they don't want to, because it might cause them some temporary discomfort (some might call it pain). But, to be clear, the client needs to go there.

As I leaned into the issue with this client, the Visionary said, "Don't go there, Mark." But, of course, I did it anyway. And I uncovered a situation where special exceptions were allotted to the daughter. No surprise. But now it was out in the open. The Sales Leader was uncomfortable, feeling doubts about raising the issue. The rest of the leadership team was asking themselves: where else is this happening? Would they be asked to make exceptions for someone else on their team?

The Visionary was now super uncomfortable. Nepotism was exposed in broad daylight. Couldn't hide from it now. What would you do in that situation?

That problem was there already. The only thing that had changed was that now everyone could see it clearly for what it was. And how could anyone say this favoritism was helping the company get closer to achieving their vision?

Care to guess what that Visionary did? Well, he danced a little bit in the session. He committed to a follow-up discussion with the parties involved. He put on a happy face and made it to the end of the day. Then, a few days later, he sent me an email; he fired me. That wasn't the reason he cited. He was a long-term client, and he expressed sentiments along the lines of "having learned what they needed."

Do you think he addressed the real issue? Or did he reinforce the idea that there are "sacred cows" we don't discuss?

Where might you be making silent exceptions right now—and what message is that sending to your team?

Your actions speak far louder than words. Remember: All eyes are on you daily.

Stop Thinking Out Loud

Your words are powerful. During an interview on Ron Lovett's *Scaling Culture* podcast, Jeffrey Immelt, former CEO of General Electric, said:

> As entrepreneurs and leaders, we're so used to thinking out loud, we need to be mindful of who we are doing it in front of. People hang off of our every word. When we're speaking out loud with our crazy ideas, this can frighten people—or worse—turn into a distracting to-do list. (Thanks to Verne Harnish for finding this.)

Your team is tuned in to whatever comes out of your mouth. They are listening closely. In a worst case, you may make a comment, and somebody runs with it, not realizing you were just thinking out loud. They start doing a bunch of things that you didn't intend at all. And suddenly, someone has spent time and effort into making your "thought" a reality. You may be shocked to discover that someone spent two weeks working on that idea you had.

Likewise, when you voice a crazy idea in front of people, it might scare them. Remember, *do no harm*.

The only way to avoid harm is for you to stop thinking out loud.

If you must think out loud, because that's just how you're hard-wired, here are two helpful mechanisms. First, label the thought. If you're ever in a group and feel the urge to think out loud, tell them, "Everyone, I'd like to think out loud on this for a bit. Nobody is to take any action whatsoever on anything I'm about to say. This is for discussion only."

Second, identify a thinking partner. This is a person who fully understands that you have this pattern. They can engage in the process with you without getting alarmed. They know better than to take any related action without first confirming that this is actually a direction you're committed to. It should be no surprise that many Visionaries find their Integrator to be a great choice for this. And you can also have thinking partners from other places as well. Think back to our lists from Pillar 3: Surround Yourself. Many of those individuals could be great thinking partners for you.

Stay Out of the Trees

I'm sure you've heard the saying, "You can't see the forest for the trees." I'd like to drive that home with an example that's a little closer to your Visionary role. In her book, *Fierce Conversations*, Susan Scott introduces a concept she calls the "Decision Tree."

As Visionaries, one of the hardest things to let go of is control over decisions. We tell ourselves it's faster to just decide it ourselves. Or safer. Or smarter. But here's the truth: not every decision deserves your time or attention.

When you insert yourself into every decision, especially the ones your Integrator or team is perfectly capable of making, you create confusion, drag, and eventually, resentment.

The Decision Tree helps to clarify *which* decisions truly require your involvement and *how much*.

WHERE DOES YOUR DECISION LIVE?

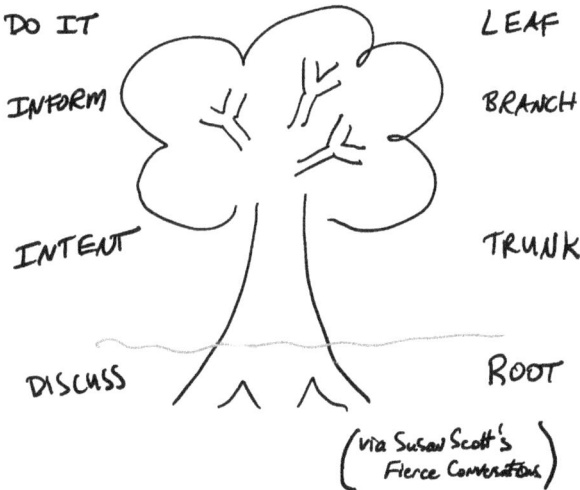

DO IT	LEAF
INFORM	BRANCH
INTENT	TRUNK
DISCUSS	ROOT

(via Susan Scott's Fierce Conversations)

Imagine a tree. At the top are the leaves, those quick, routine decisions that pose no real threat to the business. At the base are the roots: Mission-critical decisions that, if made incorrectly, could do serious harm. They're "below the waterline" and might even "sink your ship."

- Leaf-level decisions are things your people should just do. No special permission. No delay. No announcement. Just move.
- Branch-level decisions can be made independently, but they should *inform* you after the fact. This keeps you in the loop and helps you to coach them when needed.
- Trunk-level decisions require people to *announce their intent* before acting. You give yourself a window to intervene if necessary.
- Root-level decisions must be *discussed*. These are the ones that could sink the ship. No movement is permitted until alignment is reached.

That one-word expectation—**do**, **inform**, **intent**, or **discuss**—becomes the guidepost for how your team handles every level of decision. And when your Integrator uses this language with their own direct reports, it cascades clarity throughout the organization.

One of my clients—a classic Visionary—once told me, "I feel like I'm the human bottleneck. Everyone's waiting for me to weigh in on everything." And he was right. But when we mapped his team's decisions against this model, we found that 80 percent of them were leaf- or branch-level. Once his team had permission to move, they did, and it unlocked their true power.

The Decision Tree doesn't just protect the business. It protects your freedom, and it gives your Integrator the runway they need to lead.

You've got the gifts. You've got the team. You've got the tools. Now your job is simpler, but not easy: protect the momentum you've created. Don't second-guess it. Don't sabotage it.

Because here's the truth: when you do harm, you're not just hurting your team, you're limiting your own freedom.

Every time you violate trust, create confusion, or make exceptions, you're building friction into the system you're counting on to set you free.

But when you lead with clarity, consistency, and commitment. That's when the flywheel turns. That's when the team runs.

And that's when *your* freedom expands exponentially.

Transformation

The "Do No Harm" worksheet is another introspection exercise, where you have to be open and honest with yourself.

In the exercise below, you'll find several harmful behaviors we explored in this chapter. Start by scoring yourself on each one. The scale is 1–10, where 10 is the most harmful. As you rate each one, think of the scale like this:

One is, "Yes, I'm doing it. It's not helping, but it's not hurting."

Ten is, "Yes, I'm doing it. And, you know what? This is probably shooting our wheels off."

Reflect on what's driving your high scores. Is it ego? Impatience? Lack of awareness? Which of your actions, habits, and tendencies are currently causing the most harm? Write down any notes or possible solutions in the Mitigation column.

POTENTIAL HARM	RISK (1–10)	MITIGATION
Sending mixed signals about the vision		
Being half-in on OS, or V/I structure		
Making special exceptions		
Thinking out loud in front of the team		
Getting caught up in Leaf/Branch-level decisions		

After you've rated each one, sit back and study that entire list, along with the ratings you selected. From that view, what's the one harm you see that stands out? You want to uncover the one harm that, if you could really make a change, would unlock the most opportunity. Are you willing to do it? If not, what's holding you back? Whatever the answer is, is that more important than moving toward your vision?

Hmmmm. It's a big question. Too often, I watch a Visionary make a short-term, ego-driven choice, which feels good to them in the moment. Yet they sacrifice their long-term vision in the process, sometimes to great detriment. As a fellow EOS Implementer once pointed out to me, "They're screwing up the single largest investment in their entire portfolio."

Whatever focus you choose from this list, you must truly commit to change. If you're not committed, it won't work. So pick the thing you'll really do, even if it's not the most damaging item on the list.

Write it down. Consider sharing it with your Integrator or your Community.

Finally, step back and look at the big picture.

Are you making it easier—or harder—for your business to run without you?

Your freedom depends on that answer.

Pillar 10: Do No Harm

☐ Recognizes that avoiding harm is a leadership discipline and a prerequisite for sustainable freedom.

☐ Holds themselves accountable for consistency and clarity in vision. Make this a priority.

☐ Does not waffle or send mixed signals.

☐ Does not undermine the structure with special exemptions.

☐ Signals an "alert" when thinking out loud, so teams don't mistake it for new marching orders.

☐ Uses the Decision Tree to empower leaders to make decisions with accountability.

To round out this pillar, please get out your Visionary Report Card (VRC) and read the mindsets above that go along with Pillar 10. Give yourself Xs or slashes next to the mindsets you're doing well in, leaving blank the mindsets where you have substantial work to do. Then give yourself a rating on how well you are doing. The scale is 1 to 10, with 10 being the highest.

Moving now to conclude our journey. Let's bring it all together for you.

CONCLUSION

Do not go where the path may lead, go instead
where there is no path and leave a trail.

—*Ralph Waldo Emerson*

I often hear, "Most Visionaries have the attention span of a gnat." While largely true, if you've made it this far, you have also demonstrated a certain desire. A force inside you wants to become truly great as a Visionary.

All along during the 10 Pillars, you've been rating yourself on how well you're doing in each. Now that we've gone through all ten, it's time to tally up your total score.

PILLAR	SCORE (1–10)
1 - Know Thyself	
2 - Maintain Warrior Shape	
3 - Surround Yourself	
4 - Commit to your OS	
5 - Support Your Integrator	
6 - Think About What You Think About	
7 - Watch Out for Pitfalls	
8 - Help Others Stretch	
9 - Go Slow To Go Fast	
10 - Do No Harm	
TOTAL	

Enter your total score for each Pillar, and add them up. Keep in mind, each pillar was scored 1–10, so the highest your total could be is 100.

I trust you were completely honest with yourself along the way. Remember, if you're not honest with yourself, you'll just slow down your own opportunity for progress.

How'd you do? How does your score feel to you?

Sometimes, in a live workshop, I'll ask everyone to raise their hands if their total score is 10 or better. All hands go up—unless someone is exceptionally bad at following directions. Then I'll have them keep their hands up as I progressively raise the score. Who scored 20 or more? How about 30? 40? 50? 60 or better? Anyone score 70, 80, 90, or better?"

As you might guess, a lot of people fall in the middle, with a healthy amount of areas to work on. A few score really low, some of whom are likely being too hard on themselves. Or maybe they're in a transitional phase, where it's just hard to tell. And there's always a group that scores pretty high. Of that group, the discussion demonstrates that some truly are in a good place. It also shows us that some aren't; that is, those who aren't truly willing to be honest with themselves. They are more concerned about posting the high score and are not yet ready to grow as a Visionary.

However, we hold no judgment. Everyone is right where they are until they're ready to move.

Keep in mind that this number is your baseline. It's not your destination, it's your starting point. It's a number for you to work from.

It gives you insight into a meaty list of subjects you can discuss with your Integrator.

You can also figure out where your opportunities are for progress.

When you come to the end of the next quarter, complete the VRC again. You can track the areas where you've grown, and decide what to work on next.

Remember, you're looking for progress. Just keep chipping away at it. Little by little. Always look for progress.

And that, my friends, is your Visionary Report Card.

Do you remember how this journey started?

You picked up this book feeling lost, or maybe just tired, and you discovered the 10 Pillars. Now you've made it through all ten. You've translated their wisdom. You've uncovered the truth behind what makes you great and what gets in your way. You've faced it all with honesty, curiosity, and the courage to change.

You're no longer wandering. You're no longer stuck. You know the path.

And now it's time to walk it.

WHAT'S NEXT?

As you navigate your path to becoming truly great as a Visionary, here is a handful of quick hits:

1. Remember the 5 Rules. As you find yourself wanting to butt heads with your Integrator, remember that this is a natural byproduct of your DNA. You're both wired differently, and you're going to create friction. You'll need to work together to blend that friction into positive power.

2. Stay on top of the Rocket Fuel Power Index, as well as both the Visionary and Integrator Report Cards. Keep in touch with how you're each doing individually and how you're doing together. Let those tools be your guides. You now have a set of baseline scores, identifying opportunities for things you can work on, so do it. Put in the work. You want to drive your Power Index scores

higher and higher, bringing all those mindsets into greater alignment. You want to see those report card scores steadily increase as well.

3. Mastery is a journey. Being a Visionary is your craft, what you're uniquely gifted to do. You've made huge strides in the pursuit of mastery by reading this book and thinking through the questions. Keep trying out new ideas and going back to figure out how to do it better and better. Keep an eye on the specific goals you've set for your future, and remember, the path to mastery never ends.

4. You're not alone in all of this. Other Visionaries— just like you—are out there fighting the same fight and on a similar journey. What you'll learn from other Visionaries will add powerfully to what you've learned in this book. In fact, sometimes more so! As you go along, you'll have ideas, perspectives, and experiences that can help out other Visionaries too. Be open. Ask for assistance. Help others. The more energy you put into your peer groups, the more you'll grow. And the more you invest there when times are good, the more likely they'll have your back when things go crazy.

5. Now that you see what truly great looks like, hold yourself to that higher Visionary standard. Don't settle for falling back into old habits that fall short. When people begin to recognize you as a great Visionary, that is a real achievement. You'll become an example for others working to be truly great at this *vital* craft. And great Integrators will be drawn to you like a magnet. More great

Visionaries helping more great Integrators means more great things will happen in the world. I take entrepreneurial impact very seriously, and I hope you do as well.

6. Don't be your own worst enemy. Manage your mindset. Avoid that feeling of "out to pasture." Instead, embrace that you are employing your intrinsic genius—your God-given talent. You are providing more value to the business than ever before because you are doing what you do best. That's right where everyone who depends on you needs you to be.

7. Let your Integrator help you. They will challenge you. They will have to say no and keep you away from the shiny stuff. When you work well as a V/I Duo, that's where you'll find gold! And one of the best ways we can support you is by also supporting your Integrator. If you have an Integrator already, I encourage you to get them into one of our Integrator training programs. There are additional tools and resources available to help you both. Check out:

- VisionaryBook.com
- markcwinters.com
- markcwinters.ai (my AI clone)
- rocketfuelnow.com
- *Rocket Fuel* (with Gino Wickman)
- *Traction* by Gino Wickman

Also, just imagine all of the types of tools that you've learned in this Visionary book—translated into Integrator language—to help them better help you. That's what you'll find in my upcoming Integrator book. Stay tuned for that!

8. Stay in touch. We're always looking for ways to improve and to create more value for you. If you have ideas, suggestions, or requests, please reach out. As you have successes and experiences that you think are cool and interesting, share those with us as well. We love to hear those stories.

VisionaryBook.com

FUTURE:
BIGGER AND BRIGHTER

So, where are you headed? As Dan Sullivan often says, "You always want your future to be bigger and brighter than your past."

I can't speak for you, but "bigger and brighter" is absolutely the kind of life I'm after. What you've learned in the 10 Pillars should be regarded as a springboard that's going to launch you toward your own bigger and brighter future.

In that spirit, I want to share this picture of a former client of mine, along with a little story that goes with it.

One day, I was busy—working hard—when I happened to notice a message. And I saw this picture from Jeff.

It said: "Hello from the Appalachian Trail."

Now, if you don't know, that trail is about two thousand two hundred miles long, and it takes seven months to hike its entire length. I knew Jeff was working in chunks to complete it, sometimes taking off a month or more at a time.

He followed up that message by saying, "My Integrator's got everything under control."

You see, he was able to step away from the helm for months at a time. Can you? Would you like that freedom to pursue your passions, whatever they may be, beyond the business?

That's the picture I want you to think of when you imagine the type of unique Visionary freedom you can have and the life that you can live.

That's what *Visionary Freedom* is all about. In EOS, we call it *The EOS Life*—a life where you're:

- Doing what you love
- With people you love

- Making a huge difference
- Being compensated appropriately
- With time to pursue other passions

Sounds pretty good, right? That's what you're working toward—what becomes possible when you live the 10 Pillars and fully embrace the Visionary/Integrator structure. I've seen it firsthand.

I AM A VISIONARY

I am a Visionary
I look into the future.
I imagine what others can't see.
I initiate what others won't start.
I pursue what others deem impossible.
I am not built to do it all.
I am built to ignite the spark—
To cast the vision, rally the team,
and build the future.
I commit to the 10 Pillars.
I choose focus over frenzy.
I choose partnership over pride.
I choose impact over ego.
I lead with clarity.
I protect momentum.
I expand my freedom.
This is the path I've chosen.
This is the life I'm creating.
And I'm just getting started.

The journey is not easy, but the simple tools are at hand. The path stretches before you. You simply have to commit to it and maintain the courage to press forward.

You are a Visionary. You are the spark that ignites the flame. The one who sees what others can't. The one who dares to begin.

You stretch boundaries. You break the mold. You change the rules. You are not here to follow. You are here to lead.

But you are not meant to do it all yourself. You are meant to dream it, cast it, and build it together with your Integrator.

Never forget who you are. And never settle for anything less.

PARTING THOUGHTS

Nice job, Visionaries! You've completed the 10 Pillars, and you are well on your way to becoming truly great as a Visionary!

Before I conclude this book, I want to offer my deep and sincere gratitude to you for the hard work and attention that you've invested along the way. Doing the work, absorbing the content, thinking about it, and preparing to apply it in your world. Your participation in the Community, your questions, the insights that you share, and your interaction with one another are all noticed and greatly appreciated.

I leave you with one last parting thought. Your clarity and your confidence are now much stronger. Keep sustaining them as you continue working to drive the Rocket Fuel Power Index mindsets higher and higher in collaboration with your Integrator. That's the name of the game—just keep it going.

And remember, entrepreneurs change everything!

You are one of the most powerful and important forces that exist in the world today.

The world needs you to be great.

Go Change the World!

That is your job. It begins when you close this book.

SELECT RESOURCES

Berger, Warren. *The Book of Beautiful Questions*. London: Bloomsbury, 2019.

Csíkszentmihályi, Mihály. *Flow*. New York: Harper Perennial Modern Classics, 2009.

Goldratt, Eliyahu. *The Goal*. Great Barrington, MA: North River Press, 1992.

Goldratt. *Theory of Constraints*. Great Barrington, MA: North River Press, 1999.

Lovett, Ron. *Scaling Culture* (podcast). Apple Podcasts. https://podcasts.apple.com/ca/podcast/scaling-culture/id1505805398.

Nomura, Catherine, Julia Waller, and Shannon Waller. *Unique Ability® 2.0: Discovery*. The Strategic Coach, Inc. 2015.

Scott, Susan. *Fierce Conversations*. New York: Berkley, 2017.

Sinek, Simon. *Start with Why*. New York: Portfolio, 2009.

Sullivan, Dan. *The Gap and the Gain*. Carlsbad, CA: Hay House Business, 2021.

Wickman, Gino. The 10 Disciplines. (Mastermind) The10disciplines.com/. 2025.

Wickman, Gino. *Traction*. Dallas: BenBella Books, 2012.

Wickman, Gino and Mark C. Winters. *Rocket Fuel*. Dallas: BenBella Books, 2015.

ACKNOWLEDGMENTS

This book would not have been possible without the help and guidance of the following people. I will never be able to thank you enough for your impact on my life, my work, and this book.

My family and friends. I'm blessed to have each of you in my life.

Beth, my beautiful and strong wife, thanks for giving me the freedom to be me and pursue my entrepreneurial quests. Thanks for believing in me and being my partner throughout the journey, even when it didn't make sense. Thanks for being a great mother to our three boys.

Austin, Blake, and Carson, my amazing sons. You have changed me more than you can know. My world has meaning because of you. You've humbled me, cracked me up, terrified me, and given me renewed hope. Your pain hurts me more deeply, and your joy lifts me even higher. You make me better.

Dr. Richard L. Winters, my father, I couldn't have asked for a better role model. Thanks for showing me the path to a life of purpose. Thanks for always believing in me and telling me "there's nothing you can't do if you'll just set your mind to it." It always felt like you really meant that, so I believed you. I miss you.

Joyce Winters, my mom. Thanks for all the little thoughtful things you did for me. And the hugs. I sure do miss those. I can't imagine a child feeling more love than I did growing up and yet you always pushed me to be my best. I still see your sweet smile from the last time I held your hand. I miss you.

Gino Wickman—my mentor, co-author, partner, and friend. You have literally changed my life. Because of you, I found my true calling and learned how to live there. You challenge me to be my best because that's what you expect from yourself. I've learned so much from you, and I suspect that's still just the tip of the iceberg.

The MCW team. Amber Baird, Integrator of Rocket Fuel, for carrying the torch. Amber Ferguson, Sarah Cirigliano, and Lindsey Pence for keeping me in LCD. Casey Stanton and Steve Caufield for helping me wrestle with marketing.

The Rocket Fuel team—Amber Baird, Sara Bagiatis, Julie Diamond, Jonathan Dornbos, Nicole Gergon, Bob Hess, Krista McCain, Kelsea Mensonides, Roxanne Ntzagawa, Lauren Shaver, and April Sonksen—for making it all work better.

The Rocket Fuel program facilitators: Rachel Downey, Haraya del Rosario-Gust, Sue Hawkes, Lisa Manning, Deb Niewald, Alan Richardson, Troy Schutte, Lesa Skipper, and Anastasia Toomey. The Visionaries and Integrators you've touched will change the world.

Other Influences: Earl Nightengale, Napoleon Hill, Stephen Covey, Dan Sullivan, Daniel Pink, Patrick Lencioni, Verne Harnish, Jim Collins, Simon Sinek, Peter Diamandis, Steven Kotler, Doug Brackmann, Jocko Willink, Ryan Holliday, David Goggins, Rob Dube, Susan Scott, and Daniel White. You've stretched my mind, and it will never be the same.

Other Contributors: Mark Abbott, Casey Cavell, Ed Escobar, Michael Morse, Jonathan Reynolds, Scott Seefeld, and Jason Williford. You've made this a better book.

Test Readers, Reviewers and Endorsers: Mark Abbott, JoBen Barkey, Amber Baird, John Burns, Tony Caldwell, Brad Croy, Alex Freytag, Chris Hallberg, Benny Fisher, Peter Hammond, Ron Johnsey, David Kaplan, Darin Klemchuk, Mark Leary, Eve Mayer, Kary Oberbrunner, Piyush Patel, Johnathan Reynolds, Will Rosellini, Indu Sanka, Brian Scudamore, John Sebastian, Ann Sheu, Lewis Schiff, Bob Shenefelt, Glen Smith, Mike Sterlacci, David Stocker, Matt Strong, Mike Sullivan, Ninad Tipnas, Christopher Turner, Carlos Vaz, Chris White, Gino Wickman, Scott Wood, and Jill Young. Thank you for all of your precious time and valuable feedback. You are forever a part of this book.

EOS Worldwide: Mark O'Donnell and Kelly Knight. Thanks for modeling a healthy V/I Duo relationship for the world to see.

Writing/Publishing: John Paine of John Paine Editorial Services. Kary Oberbrunner and the team at Igniting Souls. Thank you for helping me shape this material to effectively share it with the world.

The crew at Starbucks Lakeside, led by the amazing Kira Parker, for creating a third place that works for me. I wrote more than you know while sitting at that table.

My fellow EOS implementers (past & present): Mark Abbott, Mike Abercrombie, Matthew Abrams, Kevin Armstrong, Jeff Bain, Stas Balanevsky, Amanda Barkey, Barry Barrett, Tania Bengtsson, Greg Benson, Jeff Benton, Ben Berman, Rene Boer, Ken Bogard, Ted Bradshaw, Dean Breyley, Nate Brim, Walt Brown, Christian Bruns, Jim Bygland, Victoria Cabot, Joe Calhoon, Ed Callahan, Chris Castillo, Alexander Celie, Dawn Clarke, Lorie Clements, Jamie Cornehlsen, Justin Cox, Jim Coyle, Rani Dabrai, Daniel Davis, Elizabeth Davis, Paul Detlefs, Ken Dewitt, Sam Diaz, Marc Dispensa, Margaret Dixon, CJ Dube', Susan Dyer, Michael Erath, Beth Fahey, Ross Foca, Nathen Fox, Alex Freytag, Roy Getz, Ross Gibbs, Ben Goetz, Lisa Gonzalez, Haraya del Rosario Gust, Matt Hahne, Dan Hawkes, Sue Hawkes, Ryan Henry, Dan Heuertz, Andrea Holmes, Josh Holtzman, Stewart Hsu, Amy Johannesen, Chris Jones, Sonya Jury, Monica Justice, Angela Kalemis, Ron Kaminski, Jerry Kauffman, Jackie Kibler, Mike Kotsis, Wayne Kurzen, John Lafontsee, Jorg Lahmann, Julia Langkraehr, Patrick Lauzon, Leonard Lynskey, Jeremy Macliver, Lisa Manning, Don Maranca, Amanda Matthews, Justin Maust, Sean McDermott, Randy McDougal, Neil McLean, John McMahon, Justin Mink, Sandi Mitchell, Al Moscardelli, Daniel Moshe, Damon Neth, Clark Neuhoff, Andrew Newsom, Debra Niewald, Hank O'Donnell, Sean O'Driscoll, Mike Paton, Joe Paulsen, Erik Perkins, Dusty Pruitt, Cesar Quintero, Mary Reilly-Magee, Alan Richardson, Curtis Rippee, Gene Roberts, Jaime Robertson-Lavalle,

Sean Rosensteel, Steven Ross, Scott Rusnak, Renee Russo, Ray Salinas, Kurt Schneiber, Troy Schuette, Tzvi Schwartz, Ann Sheu, Pinches Shmaya, Bobi Siembieda, Lesa Skipper, Jonathan B Smith, Marisa Smith, Scott Smith, Tyler Smith, Shane Spillers, Dione Spiteri, Christine Spray, Brent Sprinkle, Mark Stanley, Sara B Stern, Brett Stewart, Tim Stoll, Joel Swanson, Curt Swindoll, Jack Tankersley, Jay Tankersley, Randy Taussig, Kevin Taylor, Erin Thiem, Rip Tilden, Don Tinney, Ian Tonks, Anastasia Toomey, Brian Underhill, Roger Vertannes, Michael Visentine, Jeanet Wade, Bill Wagner, Dan Wallace, Jim Wardlaw, Aaron West, Brian White, Jeff Whittle, Blake Winters, Dan Williams, Nate Wolfson, and Dan Zawacki.

And to all of my clients: I'm so grateful to be blessed with the opportunity you give me each day to do the work I love with the people I love. It is our work together that has inspired and informed this book. Thank you for being real, caring deeply, and wanting more from your business. And thank you for inviting me to share your journey. This book would not exist without you.

ABOUT THE AUTHOR

Mark C. Winters has spent more than three decades in the entrepreneurial arena, building companies from idea sketch to global enterprise. Along the way, he's started, bought, sold, or shut down fifteen different businesses. He's worked with giants like Procter & Gamble and BP, and coached hundreds of fast-growth entrepreneurial firms across numerous industries.

As co-author of the bestselling book *Rocket Fuel* with Gino Wickman, Mark introduced the world to The 5 Rules for maximizing the Visionary/Integrator™ framework. He's since delivered over 1,000 full-day EOS® workshops, founded Rocket Fuel University®, and built a thriving global community of Visionaries and Integrators learning how to work together—and win.

As a teacher, coach, and facilitator, Mark blends sharp perspective with practical process. He helps driven entrepreneurs get unstuck and expand their unique freedom—exponentially. His guidance sparks leaders to start moving, move faster, or finally move in the right direction with absolute clarity.

Mark earned his MBA at the University of Chicago, where he first caught the entrepreneurial "bug." His work has been recognized with honors such as "40 Under Forty" in both Milwaukee and Dallas, Tech Titan Emerging CEO finalist, along with Rookie of the Year and Chair Excellence awards from Vistage International.

Mark is an avid fan of college football and a long-time season ticket holder with his Oklahoma Sooners. If it's Fall, you'll likely find him with his family, in or near a stadium somewhere, fascinated by leaders and teams in pursuit of a common goal.

Learn more and connect with Mark at
markcwinters.com.

ACCESS YOUR FREE
BOOK BONUSES

ENJOY EXCLUSIVE CONTENT,
VIDEOS, THINKING TOOLS,
COMMUNITY, COACHING
OPPORTUNITIES, AND MORE

VISIONARYBOOK.COM

EOS®
ENTREPRENEURIAL OPERATING SYSTEM®

GET A GRIP ON YOUR BUSINESS

WITH THE ENTREPRENEURIAL OPERATING SYSTEM®

EOSWorldwide.com